RUNAWAY
HORSE

GREG NELSON

ISBN 978-0-692-88104-0

First Printing March 2017 / Printed in the United States of America

Hanging on with all my might,
I ride this horse . . . Life.
Powerless to control its stallion
course, yet even in my weakness I
feel God's presence as I race headlong
into that mighty wind.

To my beautiful wife
Pamela Kay (Mary) Wetch Nelson

My champion, companion, counsel,
and the love of my life.

CONTENTS

INTRODUCTION

I believe we all need a sense of place, a place where we belong. Some find it in the place of their birth; some find it where they finally settle; but our heart speaks clearly and in the listening, the matter is settled. No one—nothing else—can make that determination.

For me, the music began in Bismarck, North Dakota. I was shaped, groomed, and lavished with opportunity in this beautiful city. Her people, the leaders, schools, teachers, clergy, businesses, art, medicine, music, theater, and the history of this community are an indelible imprint on my soul. My lineage is one of farmers and fields washed in the lore of Theodore Roosevelt, Sakakawea, George Armstrong Custer, visionaries, and great political leaders who helped shape North Dakota.

Nature rests on these plains, buttes, rolling hills, and to the west, the spectacular Badlands. Harvest bursts into a vision of golden wheat landscapes, combines, and cattle grazing on the horizon amidst sky blue flax in bloom. The wild prairie rose dances among daisies and dandelions. Sunflowers follow the sun; morning facing east, evening bowing west.

This is the sacred ground of splendidly proud Indian nations, with a heartbreaking continuum of broken promises and lasting scars.

It is home to Scandinavian immigrants, Germans from Russia and many other places, and most every faith worships here. Living on the prairie has shaped every note I've written and influenced every performance or production I've created, whether in a South American village or the finest recording facilities around the world. And with that, the prairie land beckons, and I'm compelled to return for a time. That visit is sometimes physical, but more often in reflection and gratitude. These stories are my remembrances (with poetic license, but still true).

My father loved horses and one Christmas he bought me a little Welsh pony. We enjoyed riding together in a field north of the city. Time and time again I would plead with him to let me ride his prize palomino quarter horse named "Cheyenne." Burned in my mind is the day when he finally said yes and handed me the reins to his spirited gelding. Without a thought, I eagerly mounted this powerhouse and just like that he took off in a sudden burst. I almost fell off. This animal would not be deterred and he ran unrestrained on the uneven field. I thought I was going to die because I could not hold him back. I struggled and struggled with all the might a skinny little twelve year old could muster. Thankfully, after what seemed to be an eternity, Cheyenne got the message and began to slow.

When we finally came to a complete stop, my heart was pounding as I jumped off. I looked at his sweat-foamed neck, wild eyes, and flared nose. I knew I had to get him calmed down. I wanted to walk him back across the field rather than ride, but I didn't want my dad think I was a wimp. I put my foot in the stirrup, lifted myself over this magnificent horse, and this time held the reins tightly, more confident in handling him.

Looking back, I realized this runaway horse was really a metaphor for what I'd deal with in later life: fragility, exhilaration, and fear. I knew from that day forward, I would never ride my little pony again.

The stallion that would be my life would take me on a ride I could never have imagined. This would be an adventure of new seasons, new opportunities, and the process of becoming . . . and always . . . with God teaching.

—Greg Nelson

1

MY HOMETOWN

Until the arrival of white settlers, Mandan Native Americans had been the first inhabitants of the land encompassing what would become Bismarck. In 1872 the city was founded at what was then called Missouri Crossing, so named because the Lewis and Clark Expedition crossed the Missouri river there. However in 1873, the Northern Pacific Railway renamed the city Bismarck in honor of German chancellor Otto von Bismarck in hopes of attracting German settlers to the area and German investment to the railroad. Teddy Roosevelt briefly left political life in New York to ranch near Medora, North Dakota, from 1884-1886. He came to the Dakotas to recover from the death of his wife and mother.

The discovery of gold in the nearby Black Hills was the real impetus for growth. Bismarck emerged as a freight-shipping center on the "Custer Route" from the Black Hills. In 1883 Bismarck became the capital of the Dakota Territory (a combination of North and South Dakota), then later the capital of North Dakota when it became a state in 1889. Today, the state has a population of about 689,000. North Dakota is primarily a farming state, leading the country in the production of spring wheat.

Bismarck is on the east bank of the Missouri River, directly across the river from the smaller sister city, Mandan. On the west side of Bismarck you cross the Missouri River via the Memorial Bridge. After crossing the bridge and before entering Mandan, there is a five-mile stretch called "The Strip." When I was growing up, along The Strip were fine dining establishments like Jerry's Supper

Club and the Gourmet House. There were also businesses like Kist Livestock Auction, Midway Bowling Lanes, and the KBOM radio station. My dad often took me to the cattle and horse auctions and we always went to the Mandan Rodeo held once a year. Bismarck was a vibrant town that related to the arts as well, and would prove to be a valuable training ground for my life in so many areas.

2

GROWING UP IN A MUSICAL WORLD

Greater the line of preparation, the more likely to intersect with opportunity and excellence.

BOB MACKENZIE

The adventure began with my mother playing piano and marching my brother, sister, and me around in the family living room as we pounded on pots and pans. She was entirely self-taught and could play whatever she heard, especially hymns. We were encouraged to listen to classical music. Other genres of music were not forbidden, but the classics were foremost. Mom bought us basic theory books and each summer our days included daily theory homework. My older brother, Chummie (His real name is Corliss), and I would lie on the floor of a small music room that contained a Baldwin organ and listen incessantly to Igor Oistrakh play the "Introduction and Rondo et Capriccioso" by Saint-Saens. We'd get up and pretend we were playing or conducting with all the fervor our little seven- and nine-year-old bodies could muster. I was spellbound at hearing the beauty of cellist Pablo Casals playing as he groaned through many of his recordings with the Prades Festival Orchestra.

We also listened to our dad's recordings of Tex Ritter and "Sons of the Pioneers."

Later, I studied Dave Brubeck's "Take Five" and "Blue Rondo ala Turk," Howard Robert's *"Guilty,"* Antonio Carlos Jobim's *"Wave,"* and pop recordings of the day. We took our initial piano and theory instruction from our mother.

We could be playing baseball on the field behind our house and Mom would ring a bell that was our call to practice. Practice was mandatory and though I disliked much of the material I was given, I absolutely loved sitting at the piano and letting my hands take me on beautiful musical adventures that were impassioned and unrestrained. There was no question that music was in my blood. It was the constant undercurrent of everything I enjoyed.

Each musical experience was a stepping-stone, whether playing piano recitals, going to civic music concerts, Thursday music events, rehearsing, or performing in the grade school orchestra programs through high school, playing in our family trio with my brother and sister, performing with special ensembles for weddings, pancake suppers, lutefisk dinners, special programs, singing in church choir, or participating in the annual community presentation of "The Messiah" at Christmas. I loved going to concerts of visiting professional classical singers, instrumentalists, and troupes performing at the Bismarck Auditorium. My brother and I made paper airplanes out of our concert programs, and sometime during the performance, a floating airship from the balcony would come to rest on the main floor of the auditorium. Mom and Dad did the best they could with us, but it was futile.

At one of these events, a local cultural leader, I won't mention her name, came up to me before a concert one evening and looked squarely into my eleven-year-old eyes and said quietly, "Don't . . . just . . . don't," and walked away.

Okay, I'll spill it; it was Belle Mehus, the owner of the piano conservatory where I took lessons. Belle moved from the sophistication of the east to Bismarck, established her piano studio, and became a musical icon in the heartbeat of our town.

For heaven's sake, they changed the name of the Bismarck City Auditorium to the Belle Mehus Auditorium—if that gives you any sense of how she was revered in our community. I just didn't understand why she was unable to appreciate the artistic work that went into one of our paper airplanes, complete with discreet takeoffs and quiet landings.

Looking back at my shaky relationship with Miss Mehus, I don't really blame her for the warning, because she knew what I was capable of doing. I had already burned a hole in her oriental rug smoking a cigarette I found in an adjacent piano studio while my mom was with my little sister at her lesson. I had never smoked a cigarette before and I was eager to give it a whirl. I lit it, burned my finger on the match, and start coughing and hacking. Yep, I inhaled, albeit inadvertently. Frightened that I had been too loud and nervous about getting caught, I dropped the cigarette on the floor and tried to stomp it out. It persisted in smoldering, so I tried to spit on it, but I kept missing. I ran into the nearby bathroom and put some water in my hand. As I ran out I heard my mother coming for me. I just dumped the water in my hand on the cigarette and closed the door. The teacher in that studio was a smoker and so the smell of smoke didn't raise any red flags with Mom. With my best efforts at a thoughtful cover-up gone awry, the damage was done.

Later that evening, my parents received a phone call from Miss Mehus, and I was called to the phone. I walked slowly down the hall where my mother was holding the phone. She would not look at me. I took the phone and meekly said, "Hello."

On the other end of the line, Miss Mehus calmly confronted me with a description of the crime scene, complete with empirical evidence. I quickly confessed and profusely apologized. "Thank you for your apology, Greg, may I speak to your mother?" Mom spoke briefly to Miss Mehus and hung up the phone. That didn't go as badly as I had imagined, and I was faintly hopeful this might be viewed as a misdemeanor. But as my father came into view and heard Mom's report. A reduced sentence was an illusory muse on my part. In a matter of seconds, after throwing myself on the mercy of the parental court with the lesser offense out of reach; my father's teaching moment left me as a bleating sheep, bursting with many painfully repeated and fervent commitments to "never do that again." I was immediately sent to bed without being able to finish my homework. (Well at least there was one bright spot for me in this whole debacle.)

And just for the record, my father never chastised me in anger. He only punished me as a reminder of what could have been a greater devastation—like burning down an entire building. I always deserved much more punishment than what I received. Dad was a good man. Fair and never overzealous in his handling of punitive issues.

The musical world was infectious and I had caught the disease. I loved the smell of rosin on my bow as I sat in rehearsal after rehearsal. It was a virtual wonderland to me. I could never get too much of any part of my musical life. I attended International Music Camp on the border of North Dakota and Canada each summer.

I spent two weeks in orchestral programs; one week in choir and another week in theater programs. Later in the summer I attended Bemidji Music Camp in Bemidji, Minnesota, for another week of orchestra training. I had so many fun times in my camp experiences.

I remember sneaking out of International Music Camp (a big could-get-you-kicked-out-no-no) and running up to the Peace Garden Restaurant, buying an apple pie, slipping back into camp and selling it piece by piece for an exorbitant price to other campers relegated to the mundane food we were offered at mealtime. My surreptitious entrepreneurial ventures brought a very pretty penny.

I also recall that the Minnesota Vikings Summer Camp was held at Bemidji College at the same time as our music camp. We would watch Fran Tarkenton and other gridiron warriors gorge themselves on juicy thick steaks, luscious fruit, and huge salads that made our food taste even worse as we watched. On one occasion some of the players asked me if we had a band that could play for one of their little dinner parties. Of course I said yes, but actually there was no band. This was typical for me to say yes to something I had no idea how to accomplish.

This would be a pattern throughout my life. I was ignorantly fearless, thinking in the back recesses of what little brains I had that I could do it. I don't know for the life of me how I was driven to make those unfounded decisions. I personified the phrase, "ignorance is bliss." So, I put together a band of my friends from camp and we played, ate great hors d'oeuvres, and made a few dollars. I shouldn't divulge this, but during the break I got into a player's locker and stole his jersey. I think this would only be considered by my Catholic buddies as a venial sin.

I always check with them because without any doubt whatsoever, Catholic punishments are the harshest of any Christian religion. So for this malfeasance, I might get a little purgatory time, but I was pretty sure I wouldn't fry for it.

As the student conductor of the high school orchestra, I became interested in how different parts of the orchestral score were written and began reading Henry Mancini's, "Sounds and Scores," a textbook on orchestration. Once again, jumping into something about which I knew little, I ordered some orchestral score paper and began work on my very first orchestral arrangement, "Alone Again, Naturally," by Gilbert O'Sullivan.

This lyric moved me because the title embodied how I felt. Although I was in the middle of every kind of school, civic, and church activity, I had no sense of real belonging. Not fully realizing the depth of my loneliness, I began writing and slowly understood how my music and lyrics were a reflection of my soul. I think it was the beginning of my love affair with words and the power they could wield.

I finished the score and my orchestra director allowed it to be programmed for the spring orchestra concert. Hearing it being rehearsed opened a new musical road for me. I did not think for one moment that it was a piece of any significance, but I knew it was a new opportunity to grow as a musician. Of course, your family and friends would be encouraging, but I understood instinctively the great commitment it would take to swim in deeper waters. It would be years later before I would come to understand how God had been preparing me. But for now, I was in the early stages of becoming.

3

THE ROCK AT SUNSET PLACE

I lived on the west side of Bismarck near the Memorial Bridge. One block to the northeast there was a vacant field and along the edge of that field was Shirley Street. Our house was located on the corner and this is where I learned to ride my bike. Dad, my maternal grandfather, George, and my uncles, Viran and Howard, built our house for around 1,500 dollars. I lived there through high school. There were three other houses on the block at that time. One the other side of the vacant lot was a green, rectangular one-story stucco home that remained empty as long as I lived there. Next was the home of Bill and Audrey Hart. They had two girls, Cindy and Brenda, whom I babysat many times. There was another vacant lot and then Bob and Betty Miller's house at the opposite end of our block. They were a Catholic family and I knew their older children Mark, Nancy, and Rick. Rick became my roomie at the SAE house when we went to the University of North Dakota. He was a fine musician, who played the electric bass.

Behind these homes on Shirley Street was an open field. This lot was home to baseball, football, and general meetings of the kids in the neighborhood. We often met at "the rock." The rock was this humongous formation of smooth stone that was about four feet high and four feet wide. It was perfect for sitting and thinking. It was the birthplace of many ideas and dreams that incubated in my mind until later in my life. It was a special kind of spiritual couch where I loved to go. I got excited about my life while sitting on that rock. I cried and laughed with my friends there.

Behind the open field was a housing development called Sunset Place. All my neighborhood friends lived there. There were families, mostly Catholic, some evangelicals, and a few heathens tossed in for good measure. It was a perfect mix for doing crazy kid stuff together.

The cast of characters from Sunset Place included:

- Jerry Christianson (very cool down-in-the-dirt sort of guy . . . loved music)
- Larry Hoff (heavy German accent who, when he was mad, would shout out "horse milk" . . . that was a swear word unique to him)
- Marilyn Degan, (beautiful smile and very quiet)
- Tommy Beyers (the best athlete on the block)
- The Rasset family (Tim, Terry, Kathy and a bunch of other siblings whose names I don't recall)
- Doug and Dwight Baesler (we called them Dougie and Didget . . . great athletes. Their dad, Clarence, was foreman in my dad's construction company. They had a slight German-Russian accent)
- Timmy O'Neil (Was really into sports . . . his dad managed the movie theatres in town.)
- Peggi, Randy, and Ricky Stockert (Peggi . . . very cute)
- Delaree and Patty (Patrice) Novak (Delaree was a tomboy and street savvy.)
- Sandi Macnamars (great quiet smile)
- Cheryl Sloan (way cute and I got to dance cheek to cheek with her on the Novak's cement deck in their backyard . . . the song was "Summer Place" and it was the summer in between sixth and seventh grade. I was in love . . . often.)
- Tom Linford (He was older and really didn't play with us much. He was an athlete.)

- Suzanne Johnson (sweet and quiet. Her mom was always so kind to me when I came around to collect for delivering the *Bismarck Tribune*. They were in the Assemblies of God church and so I behaved myself around them.)
- There was a Mormon family further down the block . . . can't remember their name . . . but very nice . . . as you would expect.
- One of my favorite families was the Heintzman's. In that clan I knew Danny, Michael, and Kathy the best. (Great people, athletes, and had a wonderful mom and dad)

This was the day-to-day mix of characters that were game for anything. The activities ranged from playing sandlot baseball and football in "The Field," having BB gun fights (with goggles), swimming at Elks Pool, and exploring the bottomlands by the Missouri River.

Summers always held a family reunion of uncles, aunts, and cousins, many of whom were farmers. These days were also spent playing with my cousins, Doug and Judy, at Uncle Willis Alm's farm three miles south of Regan, North Dakota. We rode sheep, tried to catch birds in the grain silo, and got in Willis's way trying to help him with farm work. I thought Aunt Delores was beautiful.

If I was not at music camp, I was swimming and diving on the Bismarck Swim Team as well as working at the hospital, mowing lawns, delivering papers or helping my mother at home. It was a wonderful time in our lives during an optimum period of our country's history. The 1950's thru the 1960's were nothing short of magical. We were carefree: no locked doors, hardly any crime to speak of, and a tight community with lots of opportunities. At the time I'm sure we all thought it would last forever.

We were isolated from what was going on in the rest of the country. We saw the nightly news reports of civil rights marches and sit-ins from Walter Cronkite and the Huntley Brinkley Report, but for me the conflict did not register. I really couldn't relate to them. I never saw a person of color except one time when my father took me to the south side of town to the home of an elderly black gentleman. I think he may have been the only black man in Bismarck. It was odd for me. I'm sure my dad was trying to teach me something. Dad had a nice conversation with the man through a wire mesh fence. After introducing me to him, we left. I never saw another person of color until I went to Bismarck Junior College and we had black students from Illinois and Kentucky who played on the basketball team. I was student manager of the team.

Most of our teachers were from the North Dakota area and the gruesomeness of the situation in the south was not a matter they understood well. Subsequently, enlightenment on civil rights issues was never really conveyed with any passion—or at all—for that matter.

Oddly enough, even living in a city and a state with Native American Indians, I was ignorant as to their plight. I grew up watching westerns that portrayed Native Americans as savages who made white people circle their wagons while they tried to massacre them.

Ironically, my mother grew up at an Indian training school, which was located in what is now a military installation called Fraine Barracks. I asked her if she went to school with Native American children. She told me her father was the maintenance engineer for the Indian school and they lived on the campus. She, however, attended Bismarck public schools while the Native American students were educated at the training school.

I now feel distress that I didn't realize what the real picture was much sooner. These were nations of peoples replete with broken treaties, attempts to erase their culture, the removal of their native individual names, not having the right to speak their own language, being taken from their lands and placed on reservations thereby obliterating their entire sense of place. I always wondered how my life would change if I was the student who was thrust into another culture not my own.

4

THE DISORDERLY
ORDERLY

We were really never given an allowance per say. Our parents would dole out money only when we needed it. It was incumbent on all of us to work in some way to earn money. My brother and I had paper routes beginning in grade school. We mowed a lot of lawns and vacant lots. I hated it. I made a mental note to myself that when I got older I would never mow another lawn again if I could help it. My sister was the organist for the Christian Science Church from junior high on. My brother sang in St. Georges Episcopal Church Boys Choir for which he received twenty-five cents a week, not to mention being the proud recipient of a Jon E. Hand Warmer for perfect attendance.

When I completed ninth grade, I, for some reason, and can't tell you why, decided to work at the Bismarck Hospital during the summer months and part time throughout high school. I simply went to the hospital, volunteered, and started to work full time as a nurse's aide and then as an orderly. I loved being in an environment that helped people. It gave me immeasurable joy. I got every sort of dirty job you could get. I worked in a geriatric ward and you can just about imagine what we encountered there. My job description covered everything from cleaning up vomit and feces, turning people on their sides, bathing, applying medication for bedsores, catheterization, bringing patients to x-ray, feeding and walking patients, bringing equipment to different areas of the hospital, and preparing patients who had passed away for the funeral home.

Now if you look at these duties and think this was not optimum work, think again. I received so much wisdom from these senior members of society. They had a wealth of experience. Our conversations taught me much. I listened eagerly and was so fortunate for the opportunity to learn valuable life lessons in their presence. It was a joyful time, fulfilling and gratifying. Working in this medical universe and my time as a teacher are the only times in my life when I really felt safe, accepted, and that I belonged.

The other orderlies and I had some real fun times in this period of my life. My fellow orderly, Don, and I were always thinking up ways to have fun. We would go to a nurse's station, apply KY gel on the speaker of the handset, run up to the orderly room, and call the nurses station. We loved hearing all the varied responses of the nurses. We listened to some new combinations of words that we had never considered before . . . they had such a nice alliterative flow to them. Of course, the nurses knew who the culprits were and let's just say there were times when we were less beloved than at other times.

Our favorite pranks were visited on new orderlies. We were ruthless. One time we sent a naïve trainee down to one of the nurse's stations and told him we needed a number twenty-two inch fallopian tube and we needed it right away. We sent him off and started laughing our heads off. When he returned, he was red faced and told us we were evil. That wasn't the worst thing we did to one of our newbies. One of the doctors wanted us to take his son under our wing and show him the ropes. Boy did we comply.

Perry was slight in stature, skinny as a rail, and sported a razor thin haircut. We had just the perfect lesson for him. Don and I ordered up a shroud pack from central supply. A shroud pack was a wrapping and tags for patients who had died. The bodies were taken down to a small room, which was actually called the "paint shop."

We got a cart and Don wrapped me in the plastic shroud after attaching a tag to my toe and the outer binding. I put on some x-ray goggles before I was completely wrapped up. These goggles were the ugliest, most gaudy looking things you have ever seen. Next, Don called the young upstart and asked him for help down in the paint room. When the kid arrived, he was more than slightly nervous. Don told him that he needed to know how we did things around here and how important it was for him to learn. By this time, the guy is shaking and close to freaking out. However disingenuous, Don exuded a convincing concern for his nervous state. "Why don't you come over here next to me and I will point out a few things for you, Perry." Perry moved with faltering steps toward the shroud. "Go ahead, touch his toe," Don quietly encouraged. Perry nervously touched my toe and I wiggled it just slightly. He jumped back away from the table. "No, no, Perry. That was only a latent muscle reflex. It's no big deal."

By this time the anxiety level of this kid was exploding. "Here, Perry, I'll prove it to you." At this point Don reached up to the tie tag around my neck and loosened it. He pulled back the shroud and I immediately sat up and yelped, "HEY!!!!" It took about a minute for us to revive poor Perry and administer a little bandage on the area where he hit his head going down. He was white as a sheet. We helped him back up to the orderly room.

After that Perry didn't work with us anymore. I have to say that we were quite saddened by his decision because we had so many wonderful plans for his training. Every time we saw his dad doing rounds, we made ourselves scarce. The hospital administrator also reprimanded us for our actions. Who, by the way, was smiling during the entire censure.

5

THE FIRECRACKER CLUB

The Fourth of July was a big deal to the kids in my neighborhood because there was something magical to young boys about exploding and blowing up stuff. Don't go all psychological on me here. It was what boys liked to do . . . at least this boy. My mother told my brother and me never to cross the bridge to go to the fireworks stand. She knew us well . . . and so that's all I've got to say about that. Let's just say for now that she had great faith in us . . . to do exactly the wrong thing.

The wrong thing is exactly what my brother and I did one summer day. It was a splendiferous day filled with a sense of opportunity for adventure, mischief, and misconduct. After finding out that our mother was going shopping that day, we waited for her to leave and then promptly headed across the vacant field to the entrance of the bridge. The steel bridge had a walkway on both sides of the road. We excitedly trotted across the bridge and at the end we could see Mecca . . . Jack's Fireworks stand. Our eyes could hardly contain the wonder of the names of various firecrackers. There were black cats, cherry bombs, bottle rockets, Roman candles, and ladyfingers. Having saved our money for such a time as this . . . we literally "blew" it all. We left the stand with punks and passion, setting off our ladyfingers and black cats as we walked back across the bridge.

Cars were honking at us but we were oblivious to the danger and potential hazard we were causing. When we got back across the river, we continued our frenzied fun until arriving home. We were about to go into the house when my brother lit a cherry bomb that had a very fast fuse and almost went off in his hand. He got it off and said, "Boy that was close," and without thinking he shoved his punk into his pocket. Within a matter of seconds his pocket began exploding in quick bursts. One side of his pants was literally blown off him and he started yelling. He saw Mrs. Novak watering her flowers and he ran up to her and screamed, "Shoot me, shoot me!" She put the hose right down his pants, which gave him a brief release from the stabbing pain.

He went into the house, changed his clothes, and then went back outside to hide the blackened pants. After dinner our parents were off to a meeting at church. This gave us time to concoct a plan to explain the severe burn on his leg.

We decided to burn oil in a pan like we were making popcorn, but instead of putting popcorn in the pan we'd just let the oil burn up so we could pour a little on the floor. Everything was going fine. We poured oil in the pan and turned the heat to "high" and then went to watch a little TV while the oil was heating up. We got engrossed in the TV program we were watching and to our horror saw black smoke billowing out of the kitchen.

We ran to the stove and turned it off, but the ceilings and cabinets were completely blackened by the smoke. We did pour a little oil on the floor. When our parents got home, we were trying to wipe off the ceiling and cabinets, but we were getting nowhere. My brother used his burned leg as a distraction from the damage that was done.

The result of our handiwork was that my father had to completely redo the ceilings and replace the cabinets. We never told Mom and Dad the truth until we were adults. That incident would have to be referred to as "the worst laid plans of mice and boys." That was not the only incident involving fireworks and boyish naiveté.

One summer day I saw Jerry Christianson and Delaree Novak riding their bikes on the road by the vacant lot, so I ran up to them and ask them what they were doing. Jerry looked at Delaree, then back at my wanton, gullible eyes and smiled. "We've started a fire-cracker club and we're getting some of our favorite people to join." Surely I would qualify for this distinguished organization, and immediately asked if it would be possible for me to get in. Delaree looked at Jerry like, "I can't believe he'd do it." Jerry pressed on. "Yeah, in order to join you have to hold a ladyfinger in your hand and let it blow up.

Well, I thought to myself. *That's easy enough. It can't hurt that much. Other people have probably joined and they're alright.* (What was I thinking?) So I told them, "Go ahead, I'll join." I was such an idiot. I didn't even know what the club was about, what their goals, rules, and vision was to make the world a better place. I forgot to ask. I just held my hand out as he put the firecracker in it. He told me to close it real tight, because then I wouldn't feel it as much.

The last thing I remember as he lit the ladyfinger in my hand was a pain so great, it had to rival childbirth. I have never to this day felt anything as painful as that. I was dazed and started to stumble back to the house while Jerry and Delaree rode away laughing their heads off. Meanwhile, I couldn't understand why I couldn't feel my hand. I touched it and . . . nothing. It was still attached to my body, but it really didn't matter because I couldn't feel it.

I got to the house and tried not to let my mother know what had just happened. I awkwardly waved left-handed as I opened the screen door and walked into the house. I was trying not to cry, but I couldn't help it. It just hurt so badly. I thought I had ruined my hand and I felt so stupid.

My mother heard me and came to my room. She may have been a little scatter brained, always correcting me and expecting me to toe the line, but now she was doing for me what she never failed to do so perfectly—caring for me, loving me with words, hugs, and, "It will be better, I promise." She did for me what my dad could not understand—not that he couldn't comfort me. He had his own special way as well, but moms just have that special touch like no other.

I finally spit out what had happened, crying and nestling in her arms. "Honey, why would you let a firecracker go off in your hand? You could have damaged that hand severely." "Oh, I don't know." I guess I just wanted to belong to the club."

Mom continued. "It's alright to want to be a part of something, heaven knows I do. We all do. Maybe next time you might want to think a little more before joining." At that she gave me one of her long rolling hugs with her chin on my head. I'm recounting this some fifty-five years later. The lesson learned stuck with me. Not very many things did, but that episode in my life is something to which I always refer. "Greg, be careful what you're giving yourself to and understand just what it might cost. There is always a price . . . always.

6

MOM

M y mother was a great influence in my life. She was deeply caring, publicly cordial, extremely loving to her children, sported an underlying anxiousness, and from time to time exhibited a certain melancholy. Mom was a woman of disciplined faith and she was consistent in her spiritual walk. I held deep admiration for her on so many levels. My brother, sister, and I have somewhat differing views of her particular behaviors, but on the aforementioned, we are in complete agreement. I had some difficulty with what I perceived as criticism from Mom when it came to anything dealing with music. I felt the weight of her correction more than either my brother or sister. Whatever her faults, I loved my mother dearly.

There was no question that we could drive her nuts! Mom came from a long line of obsessive compulsives. She, like me, could be distracted very easily and was extremely forgetful. Coming home from church on Sunday was a grim experience. My mother would forget to set the timer for the roast she put in the oven before we left for church. You know that expression "Set it and forget it"? Well, our mom *never* set it and she would *always* forget it. Every Sunday we would come home to find the charred remains of said roast. We would complain to my dad and say, "My meat is too tough to eat." His reply was always the same; "It would be a lot tougher if there wasn't any."

Finally, after seeing enough carnage on his plate Sunday after Sunday, he relented and took us to eat at the Patterson Hotel restaurant. Fine dining it was—what with cheeseburgers, fries, and chocolate malts. We were in heaven.

My mother's name was Irene. I liked that name for her, it was sort of Irish and my dad used to sing "Good Night, Irene" to her in his beautiful Irish tenor voice. Unfortunately he was Norwegian, so that sort of blew that whole Irish vibe thing for me just a little. She was a kindly woman with a common properness, and always worried that our underwear was not torn or frayed in any way—just in case we were in some horrible accident and the paramedics might see us in tattered underwear. (As if the ambulance crew might see us thru the wreckage of a mangled car and blurt out, "Oh, my Lord! Did you see that? Those kids' mom let them leave home with torn underwear! I guess we won't have to be too careful with the "Jaws of Life" on this one.")

Did I mention that she was obsessive compulsive? Oh, yeah, I did. We would find her scrubbing the garage floor that she had painted or cleaning out the keyholes of our cars with Q-tips. Her mantra was "Cleanliness is next to godliness." For a good part of my growing up years I leaned a lot more toward the cleanliness part, because of some of the things I did as a kid, godliness for me was a distant goal.

And speaking of goals, I offer this parental threat level protection chart that I implemented to soften my mother's negative attention.

PARENTAL THREAT LEVELS

Level 1 (Mother snaps her fingers in the grocery store.)

No apparent danger. Feel free to continue, but act as though you are complying as long as you are in sight.

Level 2 (Mother snaps her fingers and calls out your name.)

Here there is still no apparent danger, but at this point you give her an obligatory, "I'm sorry, Mom", and a sheepish smile. This gives her the distinct impression that there is hopeful behavioral progress, though nothing could be further from the truth. You make a much greater attempt to stay out of her view.

Level 3 (Mother snaps her fingers, tells you to come to her, and makes a benign threat of some sort.)

At this point, all mischief needs to cease for at least two to three minutes, and then you are free to continue in non-compliance.

Level 4 (Mother is obviously frustrated and shouts your full name, followed by "GET OVER HERE!")

This is getting into a more murky trespass limit and certain factors must be dealt with.

1. Did she use words that she told you never to use?
2. Did she mention your dad's involvement in any way?
3. When she got home did she go to the pill cabinet and take more than two aspirin?

(At this point you are moving ... almost rushing toward level 5)

Level 5 (Mother eyes start looking vacant, hopeless, and there is a tear in her eye.)

At this point you have officially crossed the line. At this level you still hold on to the hope that you can make amends with your mom before your father gets home. This is definitely thin ice and your odds for a chance at redemption are very low. Continual contrition is suggested and helping your mom out with anything you can is a must.

Level 6 (Mom cries when your dad comes home from work.)

I think that at this point, the idea of being put into "time out" has long since passed and if you are holding out any hope for enjoying the next twenty -four hours to a week, you have definitely lost touch with reality.

Mother had a common sophistication and at the same time a confluent presence of Mr. Magoo and Aunt Clara of the TV series, "Bewitched." At home, she was either "zoned in" to what she was doing or easily befuddled. Everyone in town knew what car she drove because whenever she went anywhere, she would put her purse on top of the car to get her keys out of it. Then she would get into the car and drive off with her purse still on top. People would come up to me and say that they saw my mom and many times I would finish the sentence for them. ". . . . Yes, I know. Her purse was on top of the car." She was a notorious figure in a good-hearted way.

When she got flustered with one of us, she would rattle off all the names of her kids at once trying to identify the one she wanted. It sounded like an Asian name: "Greg-Sue-Chum!" She was certainly a piece of work.

Mom was dedicated to helping others and never considered a person's "station in life before getting involved. She was faithful to take Mrs. Klein, who was blind, to any Civic Music or Thursday Music event. She loved sweet Marie Tautfest, the lady who came to help her clean our house. There was a special bond there. Marie was diminutive and very quiet. If she spoke it was in a broken Germans-from-Russia brogue. Marie would always look at one of us with a befuddled grin wondering why Mom even asked her to come. Mom had already dusted, vacuumed, mopped, and polished the silverware so everything would look good for Marie when she arrived to clean.

In public, Mom was gentile and cordial. At home she was hard working, caring, and loving in a frenzied sort of way. I remember her taking me to sing "The Happy Wanderer" for a sixth-grade talent contest. I was so excited because I had been working on this song with my dear vocal teacher, Mrs. Moreland. Mom got into our Ford Fairlane station wagon. I jumped into the backseat and we headed off to Will-More School for the festivities. Mom was in a panic because we were late in leaving. She backed out of the driveway before I could close the back door of the car. I frantically pulled on the door, but centrifugal force finally did me in as she turned the corner in front of the house. I fell out.

As Mom jabbered away about doing my best I was flung out the back door and sent rolling onto the street. I would have loved to do my best, but it was going to be a pretty difficult thing to do lying in the middle of the street.

About five minutes later she came back and fixed her eyes on my torn pants and shirt. "Greggie! Where did you go? And how did you get so scratched up?" Well, OBVIOUSLY, I didn't go anywhere.

She continued, "I'm sorry I left without you. I was in such a hurry." Note here that she forgot that I actually *had* been in the car with her. Mom would have gone on to the school had she not remembered that she'd forgotten her tickets. That was my dear old mother, but no matter the circumstance, she was always loving and caring.

7

THIRD TEST AT ELKS POOL

W hen I was in grade school and junior high, many of my summer days were spent at the Elks Pool in Bismarck. When I went swimming, I didn't have a care in the world. You didn't worry about being abducted or kidnapped. I don't think that it was because we didn't have some really perverse people in our town, but the community's conservative lifestyle and Midwest discretion kept overt criminal action at bay to some degree. Sure, I later found out about some of the affairs that went on in the city: impropriety, closeted individuals, children living with alcoholic parents, and the general suffering of people who smiled on the outside. I took people at face value. I did not have any idea of the greater social underpinnings.

Elks Pool hours of operation went like this:

- Swimming lessons in the morning from 9–11
- General swimming from 2–5
- Family swimming from 5–7
- General swimming at night from 7–9
- Swimming from 9–10 was open to anyone 18 and older.

I would head out on my bike and ride along Memorial Highway with my towel around my shoulders and my goggles hanging on the handlebars. I could hardly wait to get to the pool. I took swimming lessons and afterward I'd walk to the park across the street and horse around with friends. We usually got a Dilly Bar from the DQ, kiddie corner from the pool, or a Lik-M-Aid from Sundahl's Jack and Jill grocery just across the street. I'd swim all day long and come home for supper after five, then beg to go back for evening swimming. My parents were always busy, so it was a wonderful time when my dad and mom would come for the five o'clock family swim hour. My dad was a farm boy and never learned how to swim and I think there was only one swimsuit he ever wore. It had black and white stripes and looked like something a prisoner would wear. Mom didn't want anyone to see her in a swimming suit, so many times we drove to Mandan to swim in that pool where she wouldn't see anyone she knew. Mom swam the breaststroke and taught me how as well. I loved this family time.

Water for me was both wonderful and frightening. When I was very young, our family took drives along the Missouri River. The road seemed so close to the river and my mother would constantly warn us never to go near the river because people drowned in that river if they got too close to it. This began my irrational fear of water. When we drove along in subsequent outings, I would literally shake for fear of the car having an accident, sending us headlong into the water. I loved to swim at the pool, but the fear of drowning and how that would be so awful was ever in my mind. In order to swim in the deep water, kids had to pass their third test in swimming lessons.

It took forever for me to even want to go near the deep end of the pool, and eventually I ratcheted up enough courage to walk over to the deep end and try to pass the test. The test was simple. All you had to do was swim the length of the pool without holding on to the side at some point. I tried so many times, but the thought of drowning overtook me and I would quickly cling to the side of the pool. Everyone else had passed this test, many who were much younger than me. It was embarrassing and every time my mother would ask me if I passed I would make an excuse about why I didn't until I finally lied and said that I had passed. For a ten-year-old kid, it was a feeling of worthlessness and somehow not being able to measure up to what the other kids could do.

Another day to try to pass this huge test loomed before me. I jumped in the deep end of the pool by the low diving board and held on to the side for dear life. I started to make the swim. I got about halfway across and once again grabbed on to the side of the pool. My heart was beating fast and I was semi frantic. Toni Woodmansee was a female lifeguard who was in high school and a mainstay at the pool.

As I held on to the side of the pool, I heard this splash and there was Toni, treading water a little ways from me. She said to me, "You really don't think you can do this; do you, buddy." I didn't answer. She told everyone near us to go away. She continued, "I got news for you. You can do this." She told me to swim to her out toward the middle of the deep water. She smiled at me and said, "I'm not going to let anything happen to you. You're safe. I'll catch you." With all the courage I had in my shriveled heart, I started to swim to her and that unrestrained fear rose up in me. I swam wildly and frantically toward her as she calmly swam up to me and held me. "See, I got you. You're okay."

She told me she wanted me to swim back to the side of the pool which for me seemed a mile away. I headed toward the side and she swam right with me. I relaxed a little more and made the journey.

Next she showed me how to tread water. She said that if I could learn to do this, I could swim as long and as far as I wanted. She demonstrated how to do it and after a few tries next to the side of the pool, I was treading water. Now I had a safety net—treading water—and my anxiousness subsided. "Go take a rest. I want you to pass this today and no more waiting," she said. I laid down on the warm pavement, water beading up on my skin and the smell of chlorine and who knows what else steaming from the cement.

Not too long after that, Toni told me it was time. "Make me proud, buddy." I jumped into the pool, this time with a resolve that

I never had before. When I left the side of the pool, I left my fears as well. I relaxed in the swim, and had no fear of sinking into the depths. I knew I could tread water and swim as far as I wanted. No big deal to anyone else. But for me, a glorious relief about which I am writing fifty-eight years later.

I am so grateful to a girl who taught me more that day than just how to make it across the pool. It really was another metaphor for many seemingly insurmountable issues that would greet me in later life. It was spiritual. It was the beginning of discovering that God uses people in difficult situations to help us either climb over, go around, go under, or go through any difficulty. Thank you, Toni, for caring for this little "insignificant" that day.

8

FRIDAY NIGHTS AND HIGH SCHOOL

I lived in an era when all my friends did a lot of things together. The dances we attended were held in various places like "The Teen Club" downtown. It was a place where we could dance and also play pool and games. There was food, candy, and pop. It was a great place for us to just hangout. There was also the high school gym, a canteen at a local swimming pool (the "Teen Canteen" located above the main offices and basket room/showers). In addition to these venues there were skating rinks and the Masonic Temple where chapters of DeMolay and Rainbow Girls held dances. Another great spot was at the G.P. Hotel in the "Four Season" ballroom. I was in heaven because they served hamburgers, fries, and pop during the entire dance. In the early sixties you might hear regional bands like the "The Unbelievable Uglies," and "The Fabulous Flippers" or local groups like "The Trade Winds Five," "Davey Bee and the Sonics," "The Dimensions," "The Marv Kary Band," and a group in which I played bass, "The Prisms." Another source of music would be groups like "Martha and the Vandellas" and other touring R&B groups coming out of Motown brought in by promoters as well as by the owner of The Teen Club.

I always got a kick out of the paper reporting any vandalism, accidents, and scuffles. They always ended or began the article by saying this incident was five blocks or ten blocks from The Teen Club. The poor owner couldn't catch a break. Yes, there were a few fights outside, but we were young and dumb and they were settled quickly and that was the end of that. It was not like today, in more "civil" times, when kids shoot, stab, and bully each other. Bullying in those days was short-lived because everyone tended to look out for each other.

The school musical performing groups had spring and fall concerts that included all grades. The choir, band, and orchestras were very good and participation in these groups was strong. Some of the smaller choral ensembles, string ensembles, and jazz bands were in demand for various functions around the city and it kept the students busy and out of trouble. There was an emphasis on theater and students could also participate in theatrical groups in the high school, junior college and the city. There was always something going on in athletics, music, theater, or service groups.

In the winter kids went ice-skating, sledding, tobogganing, and skiing at local ski slopes or cross-country. There was always ice fishing for those so inclined. There was plenty of drinking involved for many, but I got so violently sick from alcohol that I could not enjoy it. With alcoholics and addicts in my extended family it was a good thing I had such a violent reaction. It was a protection of sorts.

Friday nights were filled with football and basketball games. In between those sporting events there were movies at the Bismarck, Dakota, and Capitol Theatres in town. Fall brought football at Hughes field where the Bismarck Demons games were held.

At these football games I'd run around the bleachers with my friends and sporadically watch the game. The weather was brisk to bone chilling and warm dress was required. There was a concession stand that we kept plenty busy throughout the evening.

In grade school and junior high we were rambunctious, full of energy, and could sustain mindless play for the entire football game. In high school, homecoming was the highlight of the season, and I loved participating in building floats for the home-coming parade, going to the bonfire at the high school, and par-ticipating in the snake dance where students wound around the fire and moved together hand in hand to the football field eleven blocks away. We basked in the camaraderie and excitement sur-rounding the homecoming game. Of course there was the election and crowning of the homecoming queen, and after the game, the homecoming dance.

On wintery Friday nights I'd walk over to meet my friend, Tommy Weisser, at his house on First Street. We'd walk along Broadway avenue and its snow-crusted sidewalk until we reached Sixth Street, where basketball games were held at the Municipal Auditorium. The smell of onions and meat being cooked on a grill stopped us in our tracks at the Jack Lyon hamburger stand, kiddie corner from the Municipal Auditorium. I think the burgers were fifteen cents, and never since have I tasted anything that gave me more pleasure than my first bite with onions, pickles, ketchup, and mustard.

Tommy and I would race up the steps to the building and open the door to a magical scene where we were greeted by the sound of the pep band, led by Gordy Knaak, excited voices, and the fragrance of popcorn from the concession stand run by Adrian Dunn and staffed by kids from the school paper called the *Hi-Herald*.

Smelling that popcorn made me think of Mr. Offerdahl, my eighth grade science teacher, who told us that our sense of smell came from the olfactory nerve in our nose. He told us to think of it like a smelly old factory, which served as a great mnemonic devise to remember that particular nerve.

The players were warming up on the ends of the court, taking jump shots and practicing layups. There were bleachers on either side of the auditorium and the energy in the building was electric. When I was in junior high, I'd meet one girl at the game, talk to her, and then run down to another girl farther down the bleachers and sit with her for a time. And then there were the cute cheerleaders in their maroon and white outfits with pom-pom accessories. In high school, I knew one girl in particular. And there was something very special about her. Her name was Pam Wetch.

The officials' table was on the floor in the middle section of the bleachers on the south side of the court. The teams sat on either side. At half time the Demonette Dance Team often performed as well as the high school trampoline team. The tramp team mesmerized me, and when I got to high school, I participated on that team all three years. From the toss of the jump ball to the final buzzer, there was an ebb and flow of cheering, ranging from scattered arm chair instructions to a chaotic roar. "Defense, hands up," was the roar from the crowd. With three seconds on the clock, the end would come in a deafening triumphal exuberance or heartbreaking silence. I loved the sound of the basketball going untouched by the rim . . . *swish!* It was a beautiful sound to me.

I identified with only a few players, but none of those were the ones on the court. My players sat on the bench. They were occasionally called in as relief for the starters or if someone fouled out. I'd stare at them and see myself.

Like them, I just wanted to belong and do my best. All of my life, I never really felt like a starter, so for me the bench was not such a bad place. They'd still need me if I'd given my all to be prepared and mentally focused to fulfill my role the very best I could.

These were players who loved the game, worked as hard as they knew how to work, but were not given as much of this particular gift as were the starters. There were other gifts in their possession yet to be found. Looking back, this gives me a perspective on gifts that God gives. Sometimes in life I will start, sometimes I will wait in reserve on the bench, but as long as I give my best, there will always be a place in this life for me.

9

BOYS OF WINTER

In North Dakota winters were a way of life. There were safety procedures to deal with the freezing temperatures. You stored candles and blankets in the trunk of your car to keep warm if you were stranded. You might also have sandbags in your trunk to create traction for your vehicle. Back in the day, we used studs on tires or tire chains. It was also not uncommon to see a tall wire attached to the back of an automobile sticking straight up with a flag at the top. This was to help another driver know you were approaching an intersection where snowplows had stacked snow so high you could not see around a corner. You could, however, see the flags approaching as you came to the intersection.

If you wanted to make sure your car would start in the morning, you plugged your car into an electric head bolt heater. This heating device kept the water moving in deep freezing temperatures. Motels provided electrical outlets where travelers could plug in their head bolt heaters. Standard wear on winter days included sweaters, long underwear we called "longies," warm gloves, a parka, mittens and scarves. You had to layer what you wore. Guys could wear a cap that had earflaps that pulled down over their ears—or if the cap didn't have flaps you could wear earmuffs. Generally girls wore scarves or knitted head covering. This wasn't so much about style; it was more about not freezing your little fanny off.

I remember walking on the frozen ground delivering the *Bismarck Tribune* on my route in Highland Acres subdivision in the late afternoon. It was already getting dark and it was a lonely sound—that crunch of the snow under my rubber boots at dusk. My nose would be running like crazy, but the snot would freeze before it barely ran out of my nose.

Almost every night I hurried to finish my homework, so I could go skating at the outdoor ice skating rink. The rinks around town usually were at schools. They were about half-a-block long and wide. There was a warming house at every rink. When you put your skates on, took them off, or were just getting a little cold from skating, you could go into the little warming house. Inside you would find wooden benches around the room and a pot-bellied stove in the middle. The stove was a friend. You could put your gloves on it just for a short time to warm up. The smell of a sweaty gloves steaming on a hot stove is an aromatic recollection that lingers in my memory.

My brother and I loved to go out in the middle of the winter on overnight adventures down along the edge of the Missouri River in the treed areas of the river's overflow. We had a wonderful friend, Peanuts, our bachelor neighbor's dog. We watched Peanuts for him while he was away on business. She was a lab, retriever mix and was the most loving partner for which a young boy could wish. My brother built a little cart and we would hook Peanuts to it. She'd pull our sleeping bags and gear to our destination. When we got down by the trees near the river we'd build an igloo and forage for branches and twigs for our evening fire. Every so often we'd take a drink from the wineskin that contained our water. It was a glorious time.

Chummie and I would go down by the river bottom, find a long tree pole for both of us, put on our skates and skate among the trees on the ice of the river's overflow. We used our poles so that if we ever went through thin ice, we could pull each other out. That never happened, but we had way too many close calls. Close calls were part of the adventure for us—the unknown.

On one occasion we brought our CO2 pump BB guns and thought we might hunt. Our dad was smart in giving us these particular guns. When we went to try and shoot at a bird, you could see the trajectory of the BB as it left the barrel, and even if we did happen to hit the bird, it would just rustle its feathers and cough. One time in particular I was following my brother and tripped, shooting him squarely in the derriere. He thought I had purposely shot him and he proceeded to administer a brotherly pounding to express his feelings on the matter. After that I avoided walking behind anyone while holding a gun.

At night, a blazing fire warmed our camp while we ate hot dogs without buns and roasted marshmallows over the fire. We extracted the burning marshmallow from the flame, continually blowing on the smoldering prize, waiting for it to cool so we wouldn't burn our mouths when we popped it in. When we got sleepy, we'd zip our two sleeping bags together and have Peanuts sleep on top of us. It was heaven on earth. We took all the necessary precautions not to drink too much water at night, because the penalty for that was getting out of the sleeping bag in the middle of the icy night to answer nature's call. That for us was a real nightmare. When we got up in the morning we went exploring in the hope we'd find some driftwood we could smoke. Driftwood was very porous and after it was cleaned off a bit, it made for what I called a "Norwegian Cuban." It's amazing that I have any lining left in my throat and lungs after smoking that driftwood with who knows what in it.

Another favorite activity in winter was running rooftops and involved waiting for a heavy snowfall when snow would bank up between houses. This afforded us the opportunity to climb up on a house and run from one roof to the next. You had to be careful not to get caught, because eventually chances were you were going to put your foot right through a roof. Running rooftops was frowned upon as an appropriate winter pastime, but for the boys of winter, a most exciting mischief. After a heavy snowfall there was always the possibility of a roof collapsing under the weight of snow, so it was not unusual to see people shoveling snow off their homes as well as their driveways and sidewalks.

There was opportunity to go cross-country skiing and there was a ski area with chairlifts. It was very small. With snow-a-plenty, sledding and tobogganing were a natural sequitur and you could spend days taking the ride of your life on countless hilly sites around the town. When you said the word "blizzard" in North Dakota it meant something both ominous and exciting. Schools were seldom closed even on the coldest of winter days except when there was a blizzard on the way. Those severe storms wielded gusting winds with heavy snowfall and temperatures that could reach 50 to 60 below zero. On those rare occasions when schools were closed, kids rejoiced because it meant there would be no homework. Instead there was playing games, watching television, reading books, eating comfort food, and enjoying family. We might venture outside for short periods, but the blinding wind and bitter cold reminded us why school was out.

These blizzards were far more deadly in rural areas. I had an aunt by marriage, whose name was Hazel Miner. The story of her demise in the blizzard of 1920 is legendary in North Dakota.

Hazel was in the eighth grade and had taken her ten-year old brother, Emmet, and eight-year old sister, Myrdith, by horse and buggy to their one room schoolhouse outside of Center, North Dakota. As a blizzard developed, their school let out early and Hazel left immediately. Aware of the danger, her father had come to the school to guide his children home, but found they were already gone. Finding them in the storm was futile. Meanwhile, Hazel and her siblings kept on until in the storm they became disoriented and their buggy overturned. They laid down in a coulee and Hazel lay on top of her brother and sister. She prayed over them, sang to them, and eventually opened up her coat to further cover them. The next morning a search party found her frozen body, and when they lifted her up they found my Uncle Emmitt and my Aunt Myrdith alive. Hazel Miner is an American heroine and her heroism has been celebrated in songs and magazine articles ever since.

10

FINDING ROSEMARY

It was the summer after seventh grade and I was a pipsqueak of a kid with a high, shrill voice in full throttled constancy. My mind had the attention span of a gnat that had consumed way too much coffee. In short, I was a mess. Naïve as the day was long, I used to tell a joke I heard somewhere, and it always seemed to get a big laugh when I told my friends, but when I shared it with my youth group at church with my parents in attendance, they both suddenly started twitching, my mother covered her face with her scarf like a hijab, and both made a hurried exit. I didn't know it was a dirty joke. I didn't really even know why people laughed, but after my dad pulled me aside later, sans my mother, and told me what the punch line meant, I knew for sure my salvation was in real question.

I was a lost young boy, as lost as a young boy could be. Early in my life an adult had abused me and it left me bewildered, shamed, and secretive. I was too embarrassed to tell anyone, especially my parents. These events caused difficulties for me my entire life, and I just wish I could tell that person the consequences of their actions. As an adolescent I was constantly acting out, but always frustrated and disappointed in myself because I didn't want to hurt my parents or embarrass them.

I have lived a lifetime of sporadic anger and an effusiveness that comes from wanting to make sure everyone is okay. In retrospect I think in a way I'm seeing myself in others when I hug them, you know, like telling them they are loved and that they're safe. I'm grateful to God for walking me through the valley of the shadow; yet growing up I was unable to deal with the evil Goliath in my life. I was all alone.

I always felt like I was behind or something. I don't know exactly what I mean by that except that everyone in my class seemed older than me, you know, more mature. I was a skinny little runt with a tremendous amount of nervous energy.

I had just completed seventh grade and I didn't do too well. My math teacher didn't like me; I got an F in his math class. He made fun of me because I brought a May basket to my English teacher. He belittled me in front of the class, and I just wanted to crawl under my desk.

My English teacher's name was Mrs. Welk. She had a southern accent and that intrigued me. I really enjoyed English. I loved words and the people who used them to write stories, prose, and poems. I loved music but I was sort of lost in the wake between my talented older brother and my precocious younger sister.

On an intelligence level my great ability to be less than mediocre clearly shined. Who gets straight "unsatisfactory" report cards in first grade? My mind was always somewhere else and I could not pay attention. I wanted to focus on adverbs and dangling participles but other things in the room would get my attention, like how many squares there were on the grill of the radiator next to the windows.

"Greg, GREG!!!!! Would you like to join the rest of the class?" I would have loved to join the discussion, but I just couldn't. In high school, at the end of my sophomore year in geometry, the room was full of excitement that the school year was finally over. Mr. Huss passed out the grades, and as he came to my desk leaned over and in a hushed voice, whispered, "Greg, this is a gift. Stay in music" It was a D.

Nothing in my life had really worked for me. I was passionate, but had nowhere to release all that I felt. While I was flailing, my sister and brother were flourishing. My older brother won fifty dollars in a talent contest while he was still in grade school. He sang the role of "Amahl" in a city production of *Amahl and the Night Visitors*" and was the only freshman ever invited to be a member of the Bismarck High School Concert Choir. He started violin in the fourth grade and quickly became proficient. On the other hand, I had a pinched nerve in the wrist of my left hand. Like my brother, I began taking violin lessons in the fourth grade and the results were less than not remotely spectacular and more along the lines of tragic. My little hand would shake as I held the violin, and I managed to maintain total command of questionable intonation.

So I just get rid of my brother when he goes to junior high school, and my little sister, Sigrid, comes along. She was even worse for my fragile psyche. When she was three years old, we were driving our old Ford Fairlane across the Memorial Bridge between Bismarck and Mandan, and she began jumping up and down in the backseat (this was before seatbelts). "Drive twenty-five, Daddy, that's a B-flat" *What the heck was she talking about?* Come to find out that the hum of the bridge sounded a B-flat at precisely the speed of twenty -five miles per hour. That's how we found out that she had perfect pitch. Oh, how I hated her.

She gave her own city piano recital at age five playing Bach partitas. Later she skipped first grade. And there I was, lost in it all, caught between two siblings, who just for the record, I love like crazy but was drowning in their wake. That is when the first most life-transforming event in my life occurred.

I was sitting at Bismarck High School, waiting on the instructor for a class to teach me how to play cello. Cellos were a lot bigger than a violin and I liked how they looked, and even more, I liked their beautiful sonorous voice. I was nervous because I already failed at the violin and I was thinking this was probably going to be just another failure in a series of my life opportunities.

She walked into the orchestra room, through the chairs, music stands, and right up to me with a big smile. It was if God had sent His personal angel to attend to me. She introduced herself, we talked a little, and then she said, "Well, Greg, why don't you pick out an instrument and let's get started." Her name was Rosemary Person. Have you ever had that feeling when you knew you were in a perfect space, where the mojo felt just right, the planets were in perfect alignment and the good ju-ju was dancing all over you? Well that's how I felt at that moment. Nothing had happened yet, but the way Miss Person talked to me and introduced me to my first real soulmate—my cello, I knew something special, something otherworldly was happening. I can't really explain it, but for the first time in my life, I felt I'd met a very precious inanimate friend who would let me express my passions and deepest feelings. My fears of inadequacy, lack of ability, stupidity, and emotional fragility began to dissipate.

In just a few weeks, I was a new person. I had confidence I had never before experienced. I loved my cello and I would practice for hours upon hours, and when I got tired I'd lie down next to my cello and sleep. It was Rosemary Person who was just the right heart and professional voice I needed. I drank in her teaching, thirsty for as much as I could possibly take in at one setting. The cello for me was a perfect partner for my obsessive compulsivity and the great elixir for what seemed hopelessness to me. I realized God was giving me a gift, and it was here that I began to understand the reality of His loving pursuit.

I remember those difficult days, I remember the fear and the hurt, but I also remember the joy that comes when you find yourself, and when your Rosemary finds you.

11

GOING TO HELL IN A HANDBASKET

The colossal misunderstanding of our time is the assumption that insight will work with people who are unmotivated to change. Communication does not depend on syntax, eloquence, rhetoric or articulation . . . but on the emotional context in which the message is being heard. People can only hear you when they are moving towards you and they are not likely to when your words are pursuing them. Even the choicest words lose their power when they are used to overpower. Attitudes are the real figures of speech.

EDWIN H. FRIEDMAN

I would like to give you a perspective on the kind of thought pattern I had about God, faith, religiosity, and all things spiritual when I was growing up. Understand that in later years I have come to see that I really didn't have a grounded perspective about what I believed early on. I had strong feelings and quick answers. I find that the truths I now hold come with a price, and easy answers to difficult questions are not easy at all, except the ones that make me feel comfortable. No longer prone to cavalierly discarding or quietly belittling the views that are foreign to me, I want to keep listening and learning.

Bob Dylan explained it clearly in his song "My Back Pages." "Ah, but I was so much older then, I'm younger than that now." What I understand now is that there is a God, and I am not Him. I see that my powerlessness and my whole dependence are on His power. I have so many friends who do not hold to this idea of God or this view, but whether I agree with them or not is no qualifier to love or not love. Even more, just saying I love them, without vested action, is meaningless. I value my friends no matter our differences.

I grew up in the Evangelical United Brethren church (EUB). After merging with Methodists, EUB became the conservative wing of the United Methodist Church. In the 1950's and early 1960's no one around me was very vocal about religious matters. In Bismarck, it was understood that most every Catholic kid would go to a Catholic grade school and on to St. Mary's High School. The Protestant kids went to public grade schools, junior high school, and then Bismarck High School. We knew that Catholic kids ate fish on Fridays and also had the stopgap of purgatory, which meant an extra chance to get out of hell. Protestants didn't have this option but it seemed a great idea to a boy who had more than his share of let's say "missed opportunities" to do the right thing. In my thinking, at the time, if you were a Catholic and messed up in this life, you still had a chance to apologize. I looked it up one time to see if this was for real because I had a lot of sin on my plate and any extra help would be appreciated. So here is what I read: "Only those who die in the state of grace but have not in life reached a sufficient level of holiness can be in Purgatory, and therefore no one in Purgatory will remain forever in that state or go to hell."

Well this was a perfect scenario for me, because I certainly wasn't remotely close to any level of sufficiency in the holiness category. The down side of the Catholic Church was you had to tell a priest all the stuff you were doing that you weren't supposed to do. I was a chronic liar, so I knew I could talk myself through confession without spilling everything and letting them in on all the nasty particulars. Don't get me wrong, I realized God knew everything about me and there was absolutely no getting around that. I was constantly wondering what God was thinking about me and when He might wield the heavenly hammer.

Another concern for me was the feeling I got when I went to mass with one of my Catholic friends. It kind of gave me the shivers and a low-grade fear. I knew these guys were serious at this church because with Jesus still hanging high on the cross at the front, you could just tell those priests meant business. There was a lot of incense, kneeling, standing, and bowing; and if you ask me, I would have done exactly the same thing these Catholic kids were doing in that sort of environment. No wonder everyone was so quiet.

I went to a summer church camp each year at Lehr, North Dakota, while I was growing up. I'd accepted Jesus as my savior pretty much every summer because when the minister would ask us to look back on our life, I was positive that because of all the junk I'd done during the year, no way could my commitment from the past summer have taken. So, I would walk forward to the altar once again. I remember one of my friends saying, "Man, you get saved a lot!" I was just trying to make sure that I was going to heaven. I was full of crying and confession, but low on repentance and change.

I think there are a lot of people like that. They just want their E-ticket through the pearly gates while remaining in a life that keeps them comfortable, but no real growth past that. It was sure true of my state at the time.

I was curious about other churches in the community. Well there were plenty of Lutherans that was for sure, what with all those Norwegians and Swedes wandering around. Lutherans were an interesting lot to me. Stoic and so serious about the liturgy, they'd always sing every verse of their hymns. Didn't they ever think about singing verses 1 and 4, or even verses 1, 2, and 4 like the Methodists do? Even Presbyterians don't always sing every verse. I'm not sure about Episcopalians. Some Lutherans try to sit in the back of the church whenever they can. Actually that isn't so dumb because that way they can read a good book and occasionally nod in agreement to a random point the minister is making without making eye contact. There were Nazarenes as well and that was one crew I could never join. They had this thing called "entire sanctification," which in their words is this: "We believe that entire sanctification is that act of God, subsequent to regeneration, by which believers are made free from original sin, or depravity, and brought into a state of entire devotement to God, and the holy obedience of love made perfect." For a young kid going through puberty, this was totally out of the question.

Mormons were perfect. They didn't smoke, drink alcohol or caffeine. These people were always nice and didn't get into any trouble . . . ever. They created standards far too lofty for me. Seventh Day Adventists seemed okay to me, but I couldn't understand for the life of me why they would want to ruin their Saturdays by having to go to church. Assemblies of God and Pentecostals spoke in tongues and that, in and of itself, was a little too over-the-top for a Methodist.

There were very few Baptists in Bismarck, but just enough to make all the rest of us feel guilty. I love the joke about the difference between a Methodist and a Baptist. Answer: a Methodist will speak to you in a liquor store.

There was a Jewish Temple that all the kids in Vacation Bible School got to tour and learn more about Jewish culture. Now that was very interesting to me, but I don't think I could have joined anyway because I wasn't Jewish. I think if you want to become someone who believes in Judaism, you have to go to school and everything; and since I was already failing in the school I was in, I figured why add more misery to my life.

I guess at this point in my life I was carried along by tradition and my parents desire to have me grow up in the church. Beyond that I don't think I understood the deeper meaning of faith . . . but that would come.

12

MY FATHER

My father was raised on a farm outside Bismarck, North Dakota, in a little township called Baldwin. He had five brothers and one sister. By the time he finished eighth grade, only he and a younger brother remained with his parents on the farm. That year, his father died of a sudden heart attack, and there would be no more school for him. He and his brother took over the job of maintaining the farm with their mother. He remained there until World War II began. He was already married when he joined the army and my mother was pregnant with their first child. While stationed in the Aleutian Islands, he corresponded back and forth with Mom to choose a name. They settled on Mary Corene, a combination of both their names, Corliss and Irene. The day came, and my mother had this beautiful baby girl virtually alone. Overseas, there was unbelievable joy at reading the news of the baby's birth, and dad shared it with his buddies. After this harsh war and the completion of his tour of duty, he would have a beautiful wife and a precious new daughter at home.

It was not too long after the birth that my mother began noticing her baby's color changing and immediately secured an appointment to investigate her condition. After tests were done, the results bore devastating news. Little Mary Corene had leukemia.

It was heartrending to see pictures of my mother holding her baby and sadly smiling, obviously trying to put her best foot forward. But they were difficult, lonely steps she took. Within five short months Mary Corene passed away in her mother's arms, and my father never laid eyes on her. Mother told us of a beautiful letter he had written to her on hearing the news. After she passed away, we were going through her things and discovered that letter. My brother tried his best to read to us, but his eyes clouded up at my father's heartbroken words as he struggled to comfort his wife.

(February 1945)
A Letter from Corliss Nelson, Serving in the Aleutian Islands during World War II, To Irene Nelson, Living In Bismarck, North Dakota, Concerning the Death of Their Daughter, Mary Corene (b. September 12, 1944)

My Darling Wife,

I received the sad news last night honey, and words can't express my grief and sympathy for you dear. I know just how you feel and I want you to know that there is one person in this world, no matter how black it gets, whose thoughts are with you every moment. It seems these things just have to happen and though it seems it will be impossible to do, we will just have to brace up and try to think of the future. And speaking of that, I know you will do your part, just as you always have in the past.

I have the satisfaction of knowing she had the best mother and the best care of anyone in the world.

I'm proud of you darling, believe me, but I guess God meant it to be this way and nothing could stop it.

I went down to the Red Cross this morning to wire you a message, but I could send so few words they thought it best if I wrote you in place of it, even though it will take longer. Naturally I planned on doing that too but I wanted to say something to you and have it get there right away. They said they would let you know I got the wire, tho I felt like asking them if they weren't

*afraid it would crowd their wires too much. I know you under-
stand me my darling and know how I feel even tho I am at a loss
for words to express it and that you'll be waiting for me when I
come home to you which I hope is in the distant future.*

*Why don't you go to Minneapolis, honey, or any place for a
while? I want you to do just anything, dear, that would give you
the least bit of comfort. I'll send you every cent I can get to help
you do anything you would like. So if you can think of any place
you'd like to go or anything you'd like to do, just go ahead and
don't ask me or anyone.*

*I realize what you have done for me, sweetheart, and what-
ever I can do for you will nowhere near make up no matter what
I do. I can think of a thousand questions to ask you, but I suppose
you have already written me and told me everything so I won't
bother you with questions. Would you like to get a job, honey?*

*Please don't think I'm mentioning that for the money in-
volved, but I just thought if you think it would help you to kinda
forget our troubles and make the time go faster. It would be alright if you don't get a job that wouldn't require too much work.*

*Don't consider that too seriously, honey, because if you would
rather take a trip or do anything else that is what I want you to
do. I wish I could see you, darling. Even if only for a little while,
because I know just what kind of condition you are in and I'm
worried about you. But you will behave for me, won't you, sweetheart, and maybe before too long we can be together again so I
can take care of you. I'll try not to tease you as much as I used
to either. Really, I only did it before because I love you, which
I'm sure I always will. You said it seemed harder to write to me,
honey, than it used to be because I've been gone so long, but I wish
you wouldn't feel like that, dear, because I'm just like I was when
I left. I feel close to you, honey, and I hope you feel the same.*

*Well, darling, I've tried to put my thoughts and feeling in
this letter and it's in a rather awkward way. I know that you will
understand me and I know that I'm thinking of you and longing*

*to be with you every moment. So until tomorrow, goodnight, my
love, God bless you and keep you safe and well for me.*

Always your loving husband,
Corliss

*P. S. Honey, I have an idea you may be in Bis (Bismarck)
and this is delayed I'm awfully sorry. Bye*

I don't think the pain of that time ever left him. Some years
later, on late night drives home in our Ford Fairlane station wagon,
he would sing, "O Danny Boy." I heard the hurt in his voice as he
sang, and sometimes his beautiful Irish-tenor voice would waver
slightly, and he would wipe his eyes. Those were tender moments
and an expressive emotion we didn't see often as we grew up. His
three children could not really understand then, but somehow
were touched at the deepest of emotional levels, and the aspect of
authenticity in communicating through music was nurtured in
all three of us.

As a little boy, I'd wait for my father to get up in the morning
so I could play with him before he went to his construction job. He
would come home at noon with a sawdust face and sweat soaked
shirt. He'd eat a sandwich and as he lay down in the living room
for a short nap, I would lie down beside him and put my arm on
his shoulder. To this day, I remember how he smelled and recall
what his breath was like, his mannerisms, his temperament, what
he liked to do, and where he liked to go.

Friday night we'd watch "The Gillette Fight of the Week" and
eat a big bowl of buttered popcorn together. I cheered for the man
in the white trunks and he would take the boxer in black. On my
level, I knew this man. My life revolved around him and I loved him
like crazy. He was my protector, my comforter, and I loved living in
his house. When the neighborhood kids got together, sometimes
I'd brag about my dad. "My dad could take your dad any day," and,

"My dad is the smartest guy on our whole block." I spent time with him; talked with him, and loving him came naturally.

Often I'd ride along with him, occasionally stopping by a worksite to walk thru a newly framed house before the sheetrock was up. I could see the excitement in him as he showed me his latest construction job. He tried to get me interested in construction, but that for him was like trying to train an idiot monkey. I had no mechanical prowess and usually got in his way. He sang and I played bass together in "The Plainsmen," a group of businessmen who loved singing and performing Sons of the Pioneers material like "Cool Water" and "Tumbling Tumble Weeds." One of the songs in their concert was the hymn, "The Place Where I Worship" featuring a duet with dad and his brother, Howard.

Publicly he had a winning way about him and made friends easily. He was in demand as a soloist for weddings, funerals, and civic musical productions. We sang together in church choir. He took me to concerts, never missed any musical events in which I participated and bought me any instrument I needed, whatever it took. He'd grown up on the farm and many evenings were filled with his mother playing the organ while his brothers and sister sang together. Music was of foremost importance to him because it was music that gave life on the farm a needed relief. It was a source of great joy as they planted, harvested, and entertained themselves on cold winter nights.

Although music was important to him, he did not show much interest in any other activities in which I was involved, whether theater or the swim meets in which I participated. He was a stoic Norwegian and don't recall him ever hugging me or telling me that he loved me, but there was no question in my mind that he would do anything he could for me. At home Dad was quiet, but he was a dreamer and I think his ruminating was what I perceived as him being a little distant.

He loved making spare ribs with sauerkraut or side-pork with fried potatoes and onions. His special treat was popcorn balls.

Cooking meals and making music were good memories, and I think sharing those times with his family was of great happiness to him. As a child I didn't know the complexities of my father's life apart from what I saw. I did not realize the pressures of providing for a family and personal struggles. He had his first heart attack at age thirty and recovery took more than a year.

A man of few words, Dad was not prone to punish quickly, but when he did it was well deserved. My most cherished memory of him is this. As student conductor of the Bismarck High School Orchestra my senior year, I was on my way to conduct Tchaikovsky's "Waltz of the Flowers" from the Nutcracker Suite for our annual spring concert. It was a monumental day and my father let me drive his newly purchased Plymouth Valiant.

I took off from our house so excited, but as I turned onto the freeway I was hit broadside. It was my fault. I was not injured, but I was sick to my stomach and my head was splitting. Within a matter of minutes there were people standing around, police cars everywhere, and through the smoked filled haze I could see my father and mother driving up in our other car. Dad got out immediately and asked if I was okay. I told him I was and he said, "Go get in the car." He talked to the police for a few minutes and then came back to the car.

There was a dusking sky as I looked out my rear window and saw my father returning. There were blinking blue lights reflected on his somber face as he walked by the smoldering wreckage of the automobile for which he had saved for two years. He got into the car and just as soon as he did, my mother began, "Now, Greg . . ."

Before she could utter another word, my father motioned her not to continue. We drove on for a few minutes and then he said the most beautiful healing words ever a boy could hear, "Well, maybe you will be more careful next time."

He looked at my mother and she looked at him, without any word being spoken he was saying, "No more. That's enough." Somehow I knew that it was the end of the matter.

It would have been a perfect time to scold and berate; yet he was gentle and wise enough to know my emotional state, and just like that, mercifully released me from further humiliation. I cried and cried and cried. He never said another word about the incident. He didn't have to. He even accompanied me to my court appearance for careless driving.

When I experienced the mercy that my father extended to me, I understood that I was being spared from something I deserved. Through that experience I have learned to extend grace, which in essence is giving someone else some good thing they don't deserve. I learned both these truths from my father. That incident is so imbedded in my soul that whenever I look at a picture of him, and recall how he made me feel that night, it is a powerful influence in how I relate to God.

He was not usually a demonstrative man, but the news of my wife's pregnancy with our first child, Sarah, brought him visible joy. Two weeks before Sarah was born, we had a beautiful shower at First United Methodist Church. The next morning after the shower my father was in the coffee shop at the State Capitol of North Dakota where he served as State Superintendent of Construction. Downing his customary cup while visiting with his compatriots, he suddenly slumped over. I received a call at my home from a very alarmed and unfamiliar voice. He told me to come immediately to the hospital.

When I arrived at the hospital, my worst fears were confirmed, and for the next few minutes all I could hear was white noise as I walked the halls in an emotional haze.

Now this Norwegian Irish tenor who sang to us so many times before would not be singing anymore. He was fifty-six. The governor of our state attended his funeral and our church overflowed with his friends and family.

Just the other night I was sitting in our screened in porch with my granddaughters, Georgia, Blythe, and Tessa as they rested on my lap while my daughter, Sarah, stood near. I'd found an old recording of my dad singing, and with the ceiling fan purring above us the girls listened as their great grandfather with his Irish tenor sweetness, poured out the melody with a common plaintive passion. "On top of old Smokey, all covered with snow, I lost my true lover, come a courtin' too slow." Sarah, never before hearing her grandfather's voice, wiped her tears as she listened. Although they never met, this night brought a beautiful connection through the music.

13

CHRISTMAS

I loved Christmas up until I was about four years old. It was great getting Christmas gifts and eating the holiday goodies. But then my whole world changed as my father spoke to me one Christmas Eve. "Here, Greggie, try some of this." I tried "some of this" and almost threw up. I thought he was kidding me. Ha, ha, ha, just a fun holiday trick. Well, it wasn't a trick . . . it was lutefisk. I found out I'd have to try it every Christmas. Now Christmas Eve would become a living hell on earth. This dish made a Christmas fruitcake seem like a delicacy.

I reasoned it was the price a Norwegian boy like me must pay—kinda like penance—in order to receive your presents. I thought Christmas was supposed to be about the baby Jesus, shepherds, and stuff like that. Maybe I was suffering because I wasn't a Lutheran, I didn't know. What ever happened to, "be not dismayed"? Having to eat lutefisk was light years past being dismayed, quickly moving toward despondency and wanting to run far, far, far away—like to Fargo or some big international place like that. (Mandan was a little more doable though.)

I think in all fairness, I should at least give lutefisk a voice. Let's look at how Webster describes it:

*noun: lutefisk; **plural noun: lutefisks***

a Scandinavian dish prepared by soaking dried cod in lye to tenderize it, then skinning, boning, and boiling the fish to a gelatinous consistency.

Makes you want to run right down to the store and buy it, huh? Do I need to say anything else here? What better enticement for ladling up some "lute" and diving in. Words and phrases like, "soaked in lye"... gelatinous consistency" (remember we're talking about fish here). Uff da me! I could hardly wait... NOT!!!

There were some ways to get through it. Lefse was a lifesaver. Now lefse is akin to a tortilla, but it is made with potato, sugar, butter, and cream. And you iron it. You could put all manner of butter and sugar or jams on it and eat it like bread. Next, I'd pour all the butter I could on my lutefisk and pray that there would be plenty of my mother's Swedish meatballs, potatoes, and relish dish to get that fishy, pasty taste out of my mouth. I think here is one of the few times that Norwegian children could find some really meaningful common ground with a Swede. After all, they had to eat it too. It's kind of a Scandahuvian sort of a deal. You betcha.

Every Christmas we all got to pick out the Christmas tree, and that was quite a feat in its own right. Here's the scene. The family drives to the Christmas tree lot with three wild-eyed children all jacked up on sweets and Christmas candy registering 100 proof sugar from the time they got up in the morning. Now they're jumping up and down in the backseat, singing and talking loudly with intermittent squealing at maximum volume.

How could good parents let their children eat that many sweets? That's a very good question.

By asking that question you are assuming that our parents had any control of sweets at Christmas. Understand that we were like a pack of squirrels with hoarding issues. We socked away candy, cookies, caramel apples from every Christmas party and program that we attended. My dad would look under my sister's bed and there would be mountains of shucked sunflower seeds, half-eaten caramel apples and cookies, candy and gum wrappers, etc. I remember him on more than one occasion pulling her bed out and shouting out one of his two favorite swear words. "Judas Priest"!!!! (Note: to all the evangelicals... I know what this is a replacement word for . . . I'm not condoning my dad using that language. We should have washed his mouth out with soap!) Well, anywhoo, we had candy hidden in our suit jackets, under our mattress, in the pockets of specified pants and shirts, behind certain letters of the Encyclopedia Britannica, in dishes that were on the upper shelves and only used for Thanksgiving. I recall not being able to wear certain pants because the chocolate had melted in my pockets and I had to wait until it got a little colder because it would harden and I could then remove it. So let's just say for now, this was not a good start for Mom and Dad in trying to control our sugar intake.

At the lot, we got out of the car, scampering like mice to make our sugar-impaired choices from over one hundred trees. My parents hurriedly talked with the lot manager, grasping at any tree that would remotely suffice in order to end the bedlam of children bouncing from one tree to the next in a saccharine euphoric stupor that would have frightened Willy Wonka enough to shut down his chocolate factory. Mother is snapping her fingers, Dad is giving us the stare, but it's all for nought. I mean we were lit up like Roman candles.

The most memorable Christmas I ever had was the year that my parents informed us we would not be receiving any gifts. Instead, we would be helping out a family that had lost their farm to hail damage and were not doing well financially that year. My father heard of their plight and wanted to help. Well I must say that we were not all in one accord on this matter. In our eyes, this was the time of year when you cleaned up in the gift department, and it was a season of good cheer, joy, happiness, peace on earth, and stuff like that. Not receiving presents was not conducive to this celebration whatsoever.

Why in the world would we three Nelson kids be compelled to spread good cheer, joy, and happiness in lieu of presents? To us, the very idea was "un-Christmasy." Why couldn't Santa pick up the slack? After all, he had a reputation to uphold. My father told us that if we were helpful, we might get some little gift that year. Well, little was better than nothing, so we all complied. My dad took us out to the house (more like a hut) outside of town and we met the family.

When I walked into this shack there was only a small family room/kitchen and an adjoining bedroom. It was bitterly cold and they were using only a fireplace for heat. Remember these were North Dakota winters, need I say more? The children smiled weakly as we walked in. The parents were so grateful to my father for taking the children to get shoes. There were five children. My father had asked the owner of the local shoe store if he would sell his shoes at cost and the owner agreed. We drove to Richmond Bootery and each kid picked out the school shoes they needed.

The littlest girl caught my dad's attention as she was eyeing some engineer boots while holding her school shoes in her hand. He asked her, "Do you like those boots?" She looked at him, smiled and said, "Yes, sir."

With that he told her to go ahead and get some boots as well, and all the other children received the same. Dad was not a rich man and had to watch his money carefully, so I knew that this was a huge stretch for him. What followed was a little like out of a movie. I watched the children as they left the store. They were all looking down at their new boots as they walked out. I turned and saw my dad wiping away tears. I had never seen him cry, and I never saw him cry again. I remember leaving the store and feeling so remorseful for my selfishness. I didn't want a Christmas gift after that. I'd just received the greatest lesson of my life and everything else seemed inconsequential.

There was more to come. On Christmas Eve we opened our presents and to our utter amazement my parents had purchased a ukulele for my sister, a guitar for my brother, and an electric bass for me. We were dumbfounded at the sacrifice our mom and dad had made for us. That night, and for the first time in my life I lay in bed seriously thinking of my responsibility not only to be mindful of the hardship of others, but to act no matter the cost. As I slept, my heart was full of good cheer, happiness and joy along with the gift of understanding the meaning and reward of sacrificial giving.

14

TOMMY WEISSER

W hen I was in grade school my parents met a new family that had moved to Bismarck. They were from Norway and had been sponsored by a family here in the US. They had a boy my age whose name was Tommy. His parents, Carl and Sonya, also had two daughters, Karen and Susan, and later one more brother, Dean, would join their family.

I loved Tommy. We had so many great times together from grade school to high school. When we got into fifth grade, we both began playing violin. Later in junior high, he switched to viola and I took up the cello. We practiced together many times, attending rehearsal after rehearsal and concerts as well. We hung out on Friday and Saturday nights. Both of us got involved in rock and roll groups. He in the "Trade Winds 5" and me in the "Prisms." In his sophomore year he went back to Norway for a year. When he came back he seemed different to me. I couldn't understand what it was but I sensed it. We didn't spend as much time together and there was a melancholy to him. I would learn later that it was related to drug use.

We were on an orchestra tour to Minneapolis in our senior year and staying at a hotel in a room of about six students. Things got raucous in the banter and I was teasing Tommy . . . he kept telling me to shut up. I didn't realize how serious he was and I kept on.

Out of the blue he came over to my bed where I was resting and punched me in the face. I didn't react; I was stunned, sick, and then tearful. The tears were not from any physical hurt but from a feeling of bewilderment. The next day as we got back in the bus, he sat playing a guitar in the last long row of seats on the bus. He was playing "The House of the Rising Sun." While other kids gathered around, I watched from a distance. Life went on and we eventually spoke, but the tether of a close friendship was cut. Not because that was my desire, nor his really. We just couldn't put Humpty Dumpty back together again. That was just the way it was.

After high school Tommy virtually disappeared and no one, not even his family knew where he was. When I was around fifty-eight years old another dear friend for life, Greta, who also shared a deep love for Tommy, called me. She related that in a last ditch effort to find him; his younger brother, Dean, had contacted a former FBI agent through a family friend. No one knew if he were dead or not. It was through this effort they found he was indeed alive and the agent had located him. The abbreviated story was that after spending some time in Norway with his girlfriend and their eventual break-up, he'd, returned to the United States by working on a freighter. He got into some legal difficulties related to drugs and the draft and it sent him into anonymity. Tommy then traveled around multiple states, and eventually ended up driving a cab in Boston under an assumed name.

After I heard this news, it took a number of days and many phone calls to find his phone number in Boston. I finally made the call, but someone else answered. They went to get him on another floor because he did not have a telephone. I waited a few minutes and then I heard his voice for the first time in almost forty years. I greeted him and he seemed glad to hear from me. He briefly told me of his exploits and we laughed together for the first time in years. I told him that I missed him and how I often reminisced about our times together.

Shortly after this, Tommy moved to Minneapolis where his brother and younger sister lived. Greta lived there as well. A little while later Tommy and she were married and I went to their wedding. What a beautiful time it was. In attendance were Tom's family and Rick, my old neighbor from Shirley Street who played bass in Tommy's old band and was my roomie at the Sigma Alpha Epsilon house at the University of North Dakota. It was so great to see my beloved junior high orchestra teacher, Miss Halvorsen, as well as many of my old school friends including Danny Heintzman from my old neighborhood. This was another event I consider to be a pinnacle moment in my life and one to savor. It wasn't just the wedding, which was of a simple, beautiful elegance. For me, it was also a healing service—a coming full circle to more innocent times, and inexpressible inward joy and relief.

Through years of reflection regarding my relationship with Tommy, I see how a friendship journey doesn't always follow a strict path. For me it was a winding road, but eventually our friendship found its rest in a seasoned and resolute contentment.

15

PAM

I remember the first time I met her. She was in my American History class at Bismarck High School my junior year and she loved to debate different issues with our teacher, Miss George. I really liked Miss George and it bugged the stew out of me when this girl would banter back and forth. Finally, one day as another of these sparring matches was taking place; I turned around from my seat in the front and said, "Why don't you just shut up?" It got very quiet for a few moments, but after the bell rang I walked to the door of the classroom and waited. As the students walked out, this girl came toward the door and I stopped her. "You want to go to the movie tonight?" Without a pause, she said, "Sure," and that's how my wife, Pam, and I met.

She was one of a kind to me, confident, smart, and cute to be sure. We dated for weeks and she never gave me the green light on kissing her. Finally, in frustration one Saturday night I pulled the car over and said, "This is ridiculous, you won't even kiss me. I think I should get one at least for the last four weeks of taking you out. Again, with no pause, she said, "Okay," and I got my first kiss. She was strange that way, kind of like all business and everything. Sheesh. We went to the junior and senior proms and hung out together almost every day. The summer after our junior year she came down to Hillside Pool one morning when I was at swimming team practice and told me that her father had died the day before.

He was fifty-one. I really didn't know him that well because he was always sitting in a recliner at her home when I came to pick her up. He had emphysema and was in extremely poor health. I learned from Pam that as a boy, his brother and he slept on the dirt floor of a root cellar near the coal furnace that heated their little house on Front Street in Bismarck. He was one of six children and the history of that family was amazing. His mother and father, Stanley and Anna Marie Wetch, emigrated from Odessa, Russia, to Germany with four children, and later to the wide open prairies near Saskatchewan, Canada. All four children died of a plague right after they moved.

This is where their journey takes a bizarre twist. After the children died, Stanley took Anna Marie to Argentina with the promise of free land. During this short stay, Anna used her beautiful voice to sing in church. They came back to the United States and moved to North Dakota, where they raised six more children, Pam's father Frank being one of the six.

Pam's mother, Mae was born of Norwegian parents whose name was Spidahl. She had seven siblings: three girls and four boys. The family farmed in the Minnewaukan area near Devil's Lake, North Dakota. Mae eventually moved to Bismarck where she worked and met Frank.

Pam and I dated through high school and then she headed off for the University of North Dakota to major in speech pathology and audiology. I stayed in Bismarck and went to Bismarck Junior College. I spent my year at Bismarck Junior College working with various musical groups I'd put together and playing in musicals and chamber ensembles.

When Pam came home for the summer, we didn't see a lot of each other. I worked at a funeral home in Bismarck that summer after my first year of college.

I really loved the work because of the intriguing interaction with the families of the deceased. On the average, you spent about fifty-two total hours dealing with each client, yet only two of those hours involved the embalming process. The rest was spent making the family comfortable by facilitating funeral arrangements, handling state requirements and not so much about the macabre. I don't want to downplay the obvious weirdness of working there. Bizarre as it was, you didn't think anything of coming out of a coroner's autopsy, complete with saws and sewing tools and then going out for lunch at the Big Boy for a pizza burger flying style with onions and a "hot-n-tot" to drink.

I noticed the varied ways people dealt with death. We had people who would walk down the sidewalk on our side of the street, but when they came to our building they would cross the street and walk on the other side until they were past the funeral home. Some families would come to viewings completely drunk and others took the event in stride. Our funeral home had an organ for the services that were held there.

One evening, one of the funeral directors told me that there was no viewing that evening. I was working alone until 9:00 that night and got a little bored, so I popped up on the organ bench and was working out my version of "Proud Mary" on this little church organ. I'm jamming on this instrument as loud as I can get it when all of a sudden I hear "They've done a real good job on Marlene" WHAT? What Marlene? I jumped off the organ bench and opened the side folding door that was RIGHT next to the casket. There before me stood members of the bereaved family smiling at me.

Remember the old cartoons when someone did something stupid in the cartoon and they would superimpose a blinking sucker on the characters face? Well that's what came to mind as I sheepishly apologized for the inappropriate music being played and feebly tried to explain. The brother of the deceased came up to me and told me, "She would have gotten a big kick out of that. Don't worry".

I really thought that I would like to be a mortician, so I registered at Minot State College, which was one hundred miles north of Bismarck. When I got there, I started registering for the classes I needed to take, and to my horror found they were mostly science related. It was only then I put two and two together. They call it mortuary *science* dummy—you know—where they study the *science* of it all.

I didn't last a week there, and on Thursday morning I unregistered at Minot State College, came back home, and enrolled at Bismarck Junior College by 2:00 that same afternoon. I got a call from my dad at about 2:30 and he told me he could get me into the University of North Dakota if I wanted. Well, that didn't take me too long to decide. Pam was there and I could be with her again. So at about 3:30 that afternoon I cancelled my classes at Bismarck Junior College and went home. The next day my dad took me to Grand Forks at the University of North Dakota and I was enrolled by about 3:00 on that Friday afternoon.

I was so excited to find Pam and tell her I was there. When I finally caught up with her, she almost cried, but not in happiness. She was so livid that I had come to her school and ruined all of her fun of going out with other guys. I was oblivious to this because I thought she liked me. We dated again, but when the candidate I was championing defeated her homecoming queen candidate, we broke up and didn't see much of each other the rest of the year. What was *that* all about?

During the year at UND I met some people on campus who really clarified some spiritual questions I had. That summer I went out to an Institute of Biblical Studies at Campus Crusade for Christ headquarters in Arrowheads Springs near San Bernardino, California. It was a sobering ride to the west coast as we listened to the coverage of the Robert Kennedy assassination. It was a critical time in my life and this opportunity gave me a solid understanding about the person of Jesus Christ. I learned a lot more about myself and it was there I made a commitment to serve God for the rest of my life.

I was invited to play with Campus Crusade's traveling musical troupe called "The New Folk" and we traveled the eastern portion of the US for the next nine months. During that year we played at UND. Pam, the little Catholic girl, helped with the concert and also made a commitment to serve God in the process. She continued dating other people during this time but I wrote to her every week while I was on the road and I think a lasting love was subtly taking hold.

When I got off the road I was going to return to my college studies. It was that summer things heated up and I asked Pam's mother if I could marry her. She said yes and I could not contain my excitement. We left the house and as we drove down the street I was so excited that I stopped the car at the corner of 19th Street and Boulevard, turned to Pam, and asked her to marry me. No romance, no special planning, and no thoughtfulness whatsoever. This would begin a life for Pam with this frenetic bottle rocket.

She has loved me so deeply and has overlooked my DNA countless times. But just for the record she did not deserve my rash decision for something so monumental in both of our lives. Sadly, there are some decisions you can't take back.

Before marrying, I intended to resume my education while Pam finished her degree. However, before I could enroll for classes I was asked by the Superintendent of Schools to take a job teaching strings to fifth and sixth graders in the Bismarck School system under an emergency state certificate. In December of 1969, Pam graduated, having completed her studies in three-and-a-half years. We were married in January of 1970 at the First United Methodist church—the church my father and uncle Viran had built. It was a simple wedding and the church was full. Pam's dear uncle Gordon gave her away. Gordon and Adele have always been very special to us.

After the ceremony the reception was in the church basement. I saw that my singing group was set up on the stage as a surprise and I ended up performing with them the entire evening while the guests visited. I don't know what Pam was thinking that night but it was the musical reality this little girl who loved Elvis would live in for the rest of her life.

When we left the church that night there was a severe blizzard on our way to Fargo for a short honeymoon. As I was driving in the blinding snow, Pam kept saying, "You're going to drive us into the ditch. Let me drive." Dutifully, I stopped the car and we took off, and five minutes later *she* drove us into the ditch. We spent our honeymoon night at the Tumbleweed Motel in Jamestown, the weekend in Fargo, and got back by Sunday night to begin work on Monday. It all seemed normal to me at the time.

We spent our early years with high school students and went on orchestra, choir, and band tours. We joined a potluck group with some very special friends and even now keep in contact with them with a "round robin" letter. We also try to get together once a year. When we married we were just learning what that word "love" means . . . and we're still learning. The love we felt on our honeymoon has been transformed through years of difficulties and joys. As God continually demonstrates His love for us, that word "love" grows so much richer and deeply meaningful in our lives.

16

ROY WAGNER

We were sweating like pigs as we lay on a grassy stretch of a vacant lot. It was the summer of 1966, and my good friend, Roy Wagner, and I were taking a brief rest from a little bit of larceny involving the most perfect thumping watermelon we'd ever laid eyes on. The abduction had been a simple precision assault. I looked out for the neighbor while Roy grabbed the melon. With the prize in hand we stumbled and ran for our lives. Eight blocks later our field of dreams appeared, and we were exhausted. The smell of freshly mowed grass, a Dakota breeze, and regiments of dragonflies were all part of the set design in this outdoor sanctuary. The sun was doing her best to get a glimpse of the two thieves, but clouds kept interrupting. Life was forever and the wind was at our backs. As with any impetuous act, there was little preplanning and no utensils so Roy broke the crown jewel over his knee and we dug in with our hands. With no concern for dirty fingers, our faces bore a melon stubble while beading sweat from our foreheads exacted just the right amount of salt to flavor.

G reg, Greg, Georgia's group is coming in now." My wife summoned me away from that vacant lot of long ago and my daydreams of watermelon summers with an invitation to join her in the present.

We were at the gym at Clovercroft Elementary School waiting for a program to honor the veterans of the Army, Navy, Marines, Air Force, and Coast Guard. When we arrived at Clovercroft, young children welcomed us to the school. We walked into the office, signed in and were met by a young boy.

He looked me in the eye and nervously shook my hand. Just for a split second as I felt his tiny hand I remembered my elementary school, Will-Moore School, and the confluent aroma of milk, lunch room, floor wax, and mimeograph. He introduced himself, said his name was Lucas and asked us to follow him to the gym. As we walked he told us his father and his grandfather served in the Army. His father was a helicopter pilot. We turned a corner and came to a long hall where children were lined up on both sides of the entire length, and each held a large American flag. The tears began. We entered the gym and there was seating at the front for all of the veterans. We took our seats and saw that they had pictures of us with rank and branch of service flashing on a giant screen. As I watched the screen my mind wandered back to that summer before college with Roy and me completing our feast in the field.

When we finished our watermelon, we went over to Roy's house and sat at the kitchen table with his mother. Mrs. Wagner was a strong woman whose tanned face bore the carvings of life with a blue-collar beauty. "I love it when you boys take time for me." She smiled and then asked, "What have you been doing?"

Did she really have to ask us that question right then? Roy was fumbling for an answer but I did not hesitate. I'd been on the script writing side of many difficult questions such as this with my parents and had become adept at handling lying like an art form. "Oh, not much, we were thinking about going swimming." Note here how seamlessly and succinctly I answered the question regarding the past but quickly shifted to the future in one sentence, thus avoiding the necessity to detail our activities. Misdirection has always been a great device for any liar worth his salt.

"Well you better get over there; the pool closes at five for family swimming." We grabbed our suits and bounded out of the house. As we left his house, Roy laughed and said, "We better bring a

knife next time so we could slice the stupid melon instead of using our hands."

The next thing I knew, there was another gentle nudge from my wife in a spoken hush. "Pay attention, Greg." The program for the veterans was beautiful with the Pledge of Allegiance and the Star Spangled Banner. My sweet Georgia sang with a children's choir, and little Magnolia Blythe was on the floor with the younger children seated around the veterans. The principal gave a history of Armistice Day and Veterans Day instituted under Eisenhower. She continued with a wonderful explanation of what a soldier does and the sacrifices they make. She spoke of the hardship of battle, being away from family, going without eating or sleeping and isolation. Soldiers could be injured temporarily or for life. Many would make the ultimate sacrifice. This principal understood these realities of war because she was a member of a multi-generational family of veterans.

This profusion of fathers and grandfathers, mothers, grandmothers and children singing together took me back to the year after high school graduation in the fall of 1967.

I was with my girlfriend on a hayride, and I heard a fellow passenger say, "Did you hear about Roy Wagner?" Immediately I perked up and asked, "What about Roy?" "Well man, you know, he got killed in Viet Nam. I just stared at him, motionless. "Sorry, I thought you knew." His mom had just told me a couple months earlier that he sent her a letter and told her to tell me to "bring a knife next time," and I would know what that meant.

This would be my initiation into the reality of war and the term "soldiers in harm's way." With that all the color in my face faded away, and war for me was no longer a philosophical matter.

The choir transitioned out of a patriotic song they were singing and the choir director motioned the younger children to stand.

Everyone sang "God Bless America . . . land that I love." My response was no patriotic cliché. It was authentic and unrestrained as I looked at my granddaughters through a teary cloud. I whispered to myself through the blur of music and innocence. "Yes, Roy. I'll bring the knife, I'll bring the knife."

17

THE ARMY

O n a cold winter night in 1969, I was sitting with my parents watching their television to find out what my number was going to be in the military draft during the Viet Nam conflict. It didn't take long to find out that I would be going into the service in some branch with my number being 70 out of 366. I'd just started working for the public schools and both my immediate supervisor and the superintendent of schools were officers in the military and had the ability to get me into the Army Reserve unit in Bismarck. I wanted to serve just as my father, my uncles and my brother had done. So in January of 1970, the same month I was married, I joined the Army Reserves.

Three months later, I left Bismarck and was flown to the east coast and then bussed to Fort Dix in New Jersey. I would be thrown into a whole social universe that would enlighten this boy from Bismarck on many levels. Many of the recruits on the bus were from Pennsylvania, New Jersey, Massachusetts, and New York. I was extremely nervous with out-of-my-mind anxiety. I'll never forget what happened as I got off the bus at Fort Dix, New Jersey. We were put in rows of men from buses that had arrived earlier. There were easily two hundred recruits and we were put in four sections of fifty men each, with about ten men in each of the five rows per section.

Unfortunately I was in the front row of the fourth section. I stood next to a very heavy black fellow replete with an Afro in full blossom and sporting a boom box on his shoulder. All of a sudden a giant of a man who was no less than six-foot six or six-foot seven came walking in front of us. This black man had arms that were the size of two of my arms, sculpted like a Greek god and buffed to the absolute max. My legs started to feel weak as he began his walk along the front row, literally nose to nose with each soldier in the line. Now I'm sweating profusely and he's moving closer until he suddenly stops at the boom box man standing right next to me. He got right in his face, knocked the boom box off his shoulder smashing it to pieces, grabbed this poor guy by his fat, lifted him right off the ground and spoke quietly.

"Pretty boy, you gonna have to lose a little weight," and he released his grip. The recruit slipped to the ground moaning in agony. Well it wasn't the only thing released at that moment. My bladder was also released from duty. Falling victim to the fear of this seeming giant of a man, I wet my pants right then and there. I was shaking and feeling faint. Fortunately, he sort of walked right past me and didn't notice my "trail of fears." I was a nervous wreck.

When he got done with his inspection he pointed to one unit across from us and shouted, "Okay, listen up. Do you see these two units here? Well now that you do, know that statistics show that of the four units standing here right now, there will be one coming home in body bags. So if any of you want to screw around, not listen, and try it your way rather than the army way, this is how you will be coming home—one way or the other."

The implication of the phrase "or the other" alluded to the fact that soldiers who meant business and wanted to stay alive in Viet Nam were not about to put up with anyone who would endanger their lives in the field; so read between the lines.

When you join the military, you enter a different universe where you have little control of your world. It's kind of hard to explain, but there is a particular smell in the military. It's a cross of the uniforms, gunpowder, gasoline, and the heavy canvas on the trucks. I'll just let it go at that. The first mistake I made was responding to the drill sergeant I was assigned by saying, "Yes, sir."

He screamed at me, "What's wrong with you boy, do I look like a sir to you? I work for a living. Get down and give me fifty!"

I discovered this is not a phrase you want to hear in training. This means fifty push-ups. Okay, I thought this is no big deal; I can give him fifty push-ups pretty easily. However, I found there was one slight problem. These drill sergeants don't count in the traditional manner. Here's how they count. "One, two, three, four, five, five, five, five, four, four, five, two, three"and so on. I quickly learned who not to call "sir" as well as never volunteering for anything. It was best not to let them know that you even existed if possible. Just do what you're told and take every opportunity to keep your big mouth shut. That's what I did and it worked pretty well for me.

After we got off the bus and finished our "debutante welcome" by the master drill sergeant, we headed off to get our haircut. I felt this tap on my shoulder, "Hey, you wet your pants, huh?" I turned around and there was this skinny black man with a big smile on his face, beaming from ear to ear. "No, I just spilled some coffee on my pants." He persisted, "No way, man. Smokey scare you didn't he?"

The reference to Smokey was the Smokey the Bear type head-gear that the drill sergeants wore. "No man, it was coffee," I explained. He just wouldn't let up. "Where you get the coffee?" I didn't answer. "I see you shakin' them pants, are them nervous pants you shakin' and all?" I kept on ignoring him.

To change the subject I asked him what his name was and he said, "Bernard." I continued, "Bernard what?" "Bernard S. Dupree" was his answer." "That's a mouthful," I joked, "Well at least I don't have my pants full" he fired back, "and that for sure don't smell like no coffee to me, unless that's magic coffee. Is that magic coffee?" Exasperated I shouted, "Give it a rest, Bernard." All at once he seemed more vulnerable and said, "Man, I was just trying to have some fun, because this for sure ain't no fun here." As we stood in line for our haircuts we began to talk about where we were from and it made the time pass more quickly.

When we got to the barbershop, we found that there were three choices of haircuts. The pictures showed a haircut with a reasonable amount of hair, one that was a little shorter cut, and then an almost razor thin haircut. Bernard and I picked the first one that looked pretty good. We both got into the chairs at about the same time and the barbers began cutting our hair, but not with a scissor. They simply shaved off every semblance of hair on our head. We looked at each other and started laughing because we knew we'd been had. Everyone got the same haircut. We walked away rubbing our heads and couldn't stop laughing. It felt good to laugh because it made the stress of the unknown a little easier.

Bernie and I got to be good friends during basic. Between him, Jimmy Miller from Philly, and me our time at Fort Dix was almost doable.

Training was exhausting with marching, climbing, obstacle courses, and running for miles at a time with our full gear. I loved it when we had target practice to qualify because for just a brief period we didn't have to run. We had breaks and the common break phrase from our drill sergeant was "smoke em' if you got em'." There were two areas of training that were nerve racking and they were: being put in a dug out area with only a field instructor who ordered you to pull a pin on the grenade and throw it. This was scary territory for me; and it one of the times in training that I felt the reality of danger that awaited those who would be going to Viet Nam. The second was another exercise to crawl toward a machine gun mount as it fired actual bullets over your head. You started at the bottom of the incline that slowly rose as you crawled closer to the machine gun nest. There was no question in your mind that they were firing real ammunition because you could see the tracer bullets as they flew past your head. These were situations where people had been killed in other training cycles because they freaked out in the grenade pit. They killed both themselves and the instructor, or broke under the pressure of the machine gun fire over their heads and stood up. It was serious business for sure.

It was halfway through training that we finally got a weekend break. Bernie, Jimmy, and I were on our way to the movies and we were so excited. The movies were about the only relief we had during training and I remember the three of us singing the movie theater jingle, "Let's all go to the lobby, let's all go to the lobby, let's all go to the lobby and get ourselves a treat." We were like kids for just a little while.

As we walked to the theater, all of a sudden we saw this huge truck with a conveyor belt coming out of the back of it and other smaller trucks next to it. We stood and watched a long line of caskets being rolled out of this truck and lifted onto the smaller trucks. This is so vivid in my mind. We just stood there with our mouths open. Jimmy blurted out, "That just isn't right, huh uh, not right man." We didn't even look at each other, we just hoisted up the most respectful salute we had in us. It was a very emotional few minutes. There were a lot of things going through my mind: the reality of war and the fact that most of these heroes were just young boys and girls who had families that loved them. This was no perfunctory acknowledgement on our part; it was real and very close to home.

There was little sleep for us and we were in a constant state of training, spit polishing our boots, keeping our living area "strack" and performing various assigned duties. Even though the drill instructors were extreme taskmasters at the beginning of training, over the course of the three-month cycle we began to realize that these men were actually concerned about us. They had been to Nam and knew the realities. By the end of the three months, they'd become real friends to us. We could see how critical our training was, and what a difference it would make for those who would eventually find themselves in harm's way.

Toward the end of the cycle we went on evening exercise. On these night maneuvers, our squad marched to a specific location trying not to be identified by "the enemy." On one of these occasions we had the goofiest point man who will remain nameless in case he's still alive.

While we were quietly moving down a trail, this soldier heard something in the quiet and yelled, "Halt, who goes there?' Now that statement is not for a night patrol. It is a phrase used when you are doing guard duty. No more had he spoken those words than Bernie and I heard a huge BOOM behind us. In an instant the sky was lit up with massive flares, the sound of simulated grenades and machine guns began. Bernie and I were completely disoriented. We dropped to the ground, lifted our M-16s loaded with blanks over our head and began shooting wildly with the weapon in the automatic position.

After a minute or so Bernie looked over at me with mud all over his face and uniform. I don't know why, but that struck me so funny in the middle of all the craziness that I started to laugh. Here we were, flat on the ground, holding our weapons over our heads and shooting. We had no clue what we were shooting at, and the absurdity of it all made me laugh all the more. Bernie looked at me like he was thinking this wasn't very funny, but within the next few seconds the expression on his face changed to a big smile. That night we laid on our backs in the mud, releasing all our pent up stress and anxiety while the flares and machine gun fire blasted away. How could you ever forget an experience like that?

I completed my training at Fort Hamilton in Brooklyn, New York. My MOS (Military Occupational Specialty) was 71M20, better known as a chaplain's assistant. My unit was never called up, but as intense as our training got, it could in no wise capture the horrific reality of war. I cannot possibly comprehend the bedlam that soldiers experience in the field. Only a soldier who has fought in a war can truly understand it.

I remember a little trip I took through some of the southern states a few years back. Beauty was singing to me as I drove through the mountains of Georgia, watching the leaves paint in full spectacular astonishment. I saw flags commemorating Veterans Day alongside the road. There were also crosses posted with names of soldiers who had died in World War I, World War II, Korea,

Vietnam, Iraq, and Afghanistan. But there were other strained voices from those flags reminding me why I was able to enjoy my weekend. Young boys and girls just barely out of high school losing their lives, limbs, and sanity in defense of our country.

This isn't something that was going on once upon a time. It is going on right now. How the inconceivable insanity of war makes me grieve! I am so beyond grateful for the men and women who are serving valiantly in our Armed Forces. How much does it cost for us to simply pray for these soldiers and the mothers, fathers, sisters, brothers, wives, husbands and loved ones who are left wondering, waiting, and sometimes seeing their loved ones with lifelong handicaps and conditions . . . or worst of all . . . getting a knock at their door.

PRAYER OF OUR REMEMBRANCE
Music from "Eternal Father Strong to Save"
Lyrics Greg Nelson

O Lord let all who gather here
Give thanks for freedoms we hold dear
Remembering the bravest ones
And how they suffered, lost or won
A prayer of our remembrance now
O God sustain them by your power

Now what is left when war is done?
And joy or tears remain unsung
Would mother's sacrifice and grief
Be blessings carelessly received
A prayer of our remembrance now
O God sustain us by your power

The Lord of lights, eternal flame
Comes shining in courageous ways

Steel warriors all who gave their best
Lord guide these heroes home to rest
A prayer of our remembrance now
O God sustain them by your power

O Christ who battled on a cross
Teach us to wield Your sword of love
Restore our nation in this hour
May we your Holy Word devour?
A prayer of our remembrance now
O God sustain us by your power

18

BANDS, BANDS, BANDS

Playing in a litany of different bands and ensembles afforded me rich teaching experiences before I ever entered the ranks of the professional recording industry. It was invaluable training to prepare me as a producer and songwriter.

From the time I was thirteen years old until my senior year I played in my family piano trio and a double string quartet at the high school. In high school I played with a rock and roll group called the "Prisms." Let me be the first to tell you that there was a distinct difference playing in a classical string group and the life of a rock and roll musician. There was never a net raised to protect a cellist from beer bottles thrown by drunken bar patrons who wanted their songs played first. On more than one occasion, this underage fifteen-year-old bass player would end up playing on a little tavern stage in a small North Dakota town. In one instance the bar owner did not want to risk getting in trouble with the law and would not let me play inside the bar. Well they say that necessity is the mother of invention, and it was true in this case. He opened the back door, we dragged my gear outside and that's where I played and sang all that summer night.

While I was in my first year at Bismarck Junior College, I put together a folk singing group like "The New Christy Minstrels" called the "Greenbriar Singers." During the prom season I played piano in a little jazz quartet called "The Esquire Quartet."

I recall after playing a prom in Hebron, North Dakota in 1967, we got caught in a three-day blizzard and ended up in a neighboring small town. The next two nights I slept on the floor of their small movie theater and ate my meals at the restaurant next door. What is most incredible is that this took place in the second week of May.

My college summers were spent working at Bismarck Hospital, on the local ambulance crew and later at Boelter Funeral Home. In addition to working these jobs, I also conducted, arranged, and orchestrated music for contestants in the Miss North Dakota Pageant and later for Miss North Dakota in the Miss America Pageant. This gave me an opportunity to deal with a pit orchestra as well as continue to write and study orchestration.

My sophomore year of college at the University of North Dakota, I met a Chilean musician whose name was Jaime Fernandez. He had a group called The Fernandez Three and he was looking for a string bass player. He liked the way I felt the music and there began a year of South American music from all manner of genres. Initially we went to Minneapolis one weekend to attend a college entertainment-buying event and played a showcase. This was exciting to me because the main guest artists were "The First Edition." Kenny Rogers and Mike Settle who had just left The New Christy Minstrels put this group together.

I was fortunate to play with The Fernandez Four, performing with national touring acts in the Midwest including Dionne Warwick, The Association, Sergio Mendez, and others. These were wonderful times of musical camaraderie.

Every weekend our group was picked up at the Grand Forks airport and taken to our gigs in a little six-passenger Cherokee Piper Cub airplane. We performed at major concert venues, Greek bashes, coffee houses, or whatever.

A couple of very scary things happened during this time. One in particular was on our way to Terra Haute, Indiana. Our pilot put the plane on autopilot and I was talking to him as we sat in the cockpit. Each of us got a shift with the pilot. This time as we were talking back and forth he heard a radio communication that said, "Dubuque vortac." His face went white. At some point the autopilot had stopped functioning and instead of heading toward Terra Haute, Indiana, we were actually nearing Dubuque, Iowa. Somehow I didn't feel as confident with this particular pilot at that point.

One other frightening experience was when we were landing back in Grand Forks and our plane blew a tire. We skidded off the runway and I am not ashamed to admit that I lost all control of bodily functions at that moment. However, I did not share this with my compatriots, who by the way had screamed like a bunch of little girls.

I missed so much school that year; I don't know how I survived. Maybe I didn't, I'd be the last to know. The thing I remember the most was my choral conductor at the University of North Dakota literally red-faced and livid because I'd gone on a gig and missed the annual concert. He was right. I was a total mess. At least in the subsequent years, my wife and assistants have helped me avoid repeating the same irresponsible behavior. I apologize again, Dr. Fudge.

While I was teaching, I played a steady gig at a little supper club in Bismarck with a beautiful and talented piano player whose name was Claire Vance. Actually I earned more money playing three hours, three nights a week than I did teaching school.

Pam and I would go out once a month to the Elks Club and have a steak dinner with some of the money from that supper club gig. It was a rare treat for a musician schoolteacher, but a special time for us early in our marriage.

One of my favorite groups of all time was a group of high school students and a some local musicians called "The Renaissance Singers." The times we had together were very special to me. We practiced five days a week for two hours, played many concerts and performed for a wide variety of functions. We put together a little album that was my first swing at production. Those sessions were fun, challenging, and a tremendous learning experience for me.

My life as a musician was no different than any other traveling and gigging player. Each of us has been rode hard and put up wet many a time. I may not be quoting this accurately, but the essence of it is true: "A musician is a person who throws 5,000 dollars of equipment into a 500 dollar car and will travel 50 miles for a 50 dollar gig." But even so, each opportunity brought learning, enlightenment, and lessons.

19

BISMARCK HIGH SCHOOL ORCHESTRA

The most wonderful time of my professional life was teaching at Bismarck High School. I conducted the orchestra along with classes for chamber orchestra, music appreciation, and two periods of prep band. I have been in recording projects all over the world, but none of these experiences brought me the richness of belonging and depth of caring that I had for this high school orchestra.

To backtrack a little, after completing my second year of college at the University of North Dakota I was asked to join a national Christian touring group called "The New Folk," representing "Campus Crusade for Christ" based in California. We sang and played one-nighters throughout the US for nine months and there were many interesting experiences along the way.

As a student at the University of North Dakota, I attended a Ray Charles concert and was the only white person in the balcony section where I was seated. I loved his artistry and later on when traveling with the New Folk, I was fortunate enough to meet him at a Tallahassee motel in which he and The New Folk happened to be staying. We met Ray's wife one evening and she invited us to her room. She talked about her life with him and showed us his Braille

Bible. We found her to be a very gracious and kind-hearted woman. The next morning she introduced us to Ray.

The late sixties on college campuses were years of unrest concerning the US involvement in Viet Nam. Many college protests by Students for a Democratic Society and Afro-American Society resulted in the takeover of various buildings on national college campuses. One such takeover was in April of 1969 at Cornell University. At the same time students were taking over Willard Straight Hall, we were playing in another building on campus. For me, this was a year that brought more clarity to my understanding of societal and political differences. My faith was challenged in every way, and I found myself impotent to defend what I believed. Those were soul-searching days.

When I came home, I told my father that I wanted to travel with "The New Folk" for another year. He told me he wanted me to stay in Bismarck. This was difficult for me because I had such a wonderful time traveling, and I really wanted to continue. I don't know why, but I complied with my dad's wish. This would be a very significant decision on my part, because this next chapter of my life would never have come to pass without having honored my father and his request.

After talking to my dad, I planned to go back and complete my last two years of college, however, I received a call from my high school orchestra teacher, Harold Van Huevelen, asking if I might be interested in teaching fifth and sixth grade strings for the next school year. The offer was surprising and flattering, but I didn't see how that could be accomplished without a college degree. I loved kids and thought it would be a good opportunity to get into the school system later. Hey, I'd be making 4,800 dollars a year, so I was in the chips.

I accepted and taught elementary strings for one year. Again, I was ready to finish school when the superintendent of the Bismarck School System approached me asking if I would consider taking over the high school orchestra.

I have to explain something here. As I was growing up, I had dreamed of conducting the high school orchestra someday. There had only been two previous directors in the history of the organization. I was surprised by the offer and a little befuddled. Mr. Van Huevelen was going to become the superintendent of all musical organizations for the public schools, and that left his job open. I realized that this was no answer to be made with a quick youthful reaction. It was flattering and terrifying at the same time. I was only two years older than some of the students I would be teaching. However naively, I came to my decision and accepted the challenge. I hadn't finished college and that was weighing on me. That issue soon resolved itself with a stipulation from the state that required me to complete my college studies at the same time.

My first year was a very difficult transition for the students and me. The first day of school I told the orchestra that this was going to be a new day for them and they probably may not want to be a part of this elective class because it would not feel like an elective under my leadership. There were rumblings about my expectations. Many students quit immediately and it was a highly emotional struggle for me. Deep inside I wanted the students to like me, but without discipline and hard work it would just be another day in the park. I wanted them to feel they had accomplished something, made beautiful music and struggled, so that when they presented their program no one would have to tell them they did well. They would feel the pay-off deep inside themselves.

I don't pretend to say that I was the greatest string technician or astute musical historian, but what I could give them was a well-earned sense of accomplishment, passion for the music, ownership of the music, the exhilaration of doing things together in musical deference to each other and most of all, to listen, always listen.

The next six years of my life would be joyful years, yet extremely challenging because I had other concerns going at the same time. I was still in the Army Reserves, I had two church choirs, a musical group that practiced two hours, five days a week. I was writing jingles, producing custom records, and carrying up to nineteen and twenty-one semester hours of college classes, How to balance all of this was only accomplished because of my wife. She was the guide who kept the train running. I had been a mess in college, spending my days playing in groups and earning money to pay for the classes to which I so poorly gave myself. Marriage changed all of that. God couldn't have given me a more perfect woman to marry. Pam kept my feet to the fire as I studied and kept me on a somewhat even keel through it all.

Those days of daily rehearsals, concerts, and annual tours were wonderful. I don't want to be misunderstood here. I am so appreciative of the recording industry, the awards, the level of musicianship, and camaraderie.

There were momentous opportunities like conducting for artists at the Hollywood Bowl, Greek Theater, standing in front of recording orchestras in Nashville, Los Angeles, New York, and London. It was a great gift to learn and work with some of the finest American and European session players you can imagine. I am truly grateful, really I am, but making music with those high school students was the most joyous time in my musical life. We grew up together making the best music we could at the time. We worked hard, laughed heartily, and the best part was that we were doing it together.

I was a taskmaster fed by my obsessive compulsive wiring. From time to time I held rehearsals an hour before school began and sometimes the students would make things interesting. At one early rehearsal they wore their pajamas to make a point, cautioning my driven nature. I conducted with reckless abandon to the degree that in one instance I stabbed myself with the baton in a flurry of emotion. I never heard the end of that!

We went on tours together, sometimes to Minneapolis or skiing at Red Lodge in Montana. I loved those times when I got to see another side of these kids. Of course there was always the obligatory sneaking out of their rooms and trying not to get caught. It wasn't as if they were going anywhere in particular, but just to see if they could get away with it. I'm sure there were times they were successful no matter how hard we tried to monitor their activities. All in all, the students were usually on their best behavior.

One evening we were in Minneapolis and two of our sophomore guys were walking out of their room with towels around their necks, talking excitedly. We greeted them as we passed and asked them where they were going. They quickly informed us that they saw a massage parlor around the corner from the hotel and were on their way to get a massage. They never had a massage before and they were so excited to get one.

We stopped in our tracks and tried not to overreact. We calmly informed them that it probably wasn't the best venue to visit, and left them to ponder the truism that everything we see in life is not always exactly what it seems. They decided to go swimming in the hotel pool instead. Good choice.

This was one of the few times in my life that I felt I belonged. These students were not only students, they were my friends—friends I still treasure and keep in touch with to this day. I had the best colleagues who taught band and choir. Michael Rockne and Gordon Knaak were a source of great wisdom for me and we enjoyed our times together famously. It was an idyllic time of life, and though my life was ablaze with activity. During those years I discovered so much about the creative temperament, the psychology of working with a group of musicians and my own eccentricities.

20

GRADUATION DAY AT MARY COLLEGE

To continue teaching in the school system, I had to complete my final two years of college while I taught. The only four-year opportunity in Bismarck was Mary College, a Catholic institution. I met with the registrar and found this school to be a wonderful place to finish my undergraduate studies.

I taught at the high school in the morning and went to my college classes in the afternoon. Both Mary College and the Bismarck Public School administrators were very helpful in facilitating a flexible class schedule. I met more nuns and priests than this benign evangelical could count. It was here I began taking a serious look at what I believed . . . and why.

Oddly enough, even having been nurtured in a Protestant tradition, the two most influential persons in my life of faith were Catholic nuns: Sister Thomas Welder and Sister Jude Braus. Here were two absolutely brilliant individuals. Sister Thomas was a fine musician who later became President of the University of Mary. Sister Jude Braus was a dynamic thinker with whom I was able to take a course of study in ecumenism. When you met them, you immediately knew that you had their full attention.

They were energetically curious and inquisitive, and pretense never had its way with either one. They were always hyper focused on you. When we visited, I always had the feeling that I really did matter to them. I can't recall a conversation with either of them when they talked about themselves. They were no respecter of persons. The powerful, the meek, the affluent, and the poor all sensed their humility. Their hearts wore a beautiful vestment knit in divine love. They taught me the meaning of servant leadership by example. There are no words that adequately capture the spirit and inspiring presence of these women. They were radiant leaders, friends, mentors, encouragers, motivators, educators, thinkers, and abandoned to a certain carpenter from Nazareth. Their lives flowed from His heart, and they gave their lives away with no regret, fully understanding the folly of holding on to possessions and gifts that were never theirs in the first place. Ultimately, it is the remembrance of their lives that has fueled my every kind word, thought, and action to this day.

If there was ever any doubt that I had absolutely no idea what I was doing, graduation day at Mary College should confirm that fact right here and now. Upon fulfilling the required coursework to graduate from Mary College it was time to attend the graduation ceremony. Pam and I arrived at the graduation exercises and I sat down with her. Pretty soon she turned to me and said, "Why are you here with me, you should be sitting down with the graduating class. Pretty good idea don't you think, I mean since you are the one *graduating*!"

I walked down to where the graduates were seated and sure enough there was my seat. Placed on the chair was a note card that read, "SOC SCI" and "MUSIC." I had no idea what that meant, so I went back to the area where Pam was sitting and asked her what SOC SCI meant. She said, "Honey, I have no idea, go ask Sister Thomas; she can tell you." I finally found Sister Thomas readying herself for the ceremony. I spoke to her and asked, "Sister, could you help me, I don't understand this card that is on my chair. What does this SOC SCI mean? I know that music is my major but I have no idea what this other means." She started to laugh, and rolled her eyes. "Oh, Greg, MUSIC is not your major. We don't have a music major. Music is your minor. SOC SCI stands for social science, that's your major." Once again I went back to Pam, and upon hearing of my discovery she gave me a most incredulous look followed by, "Oh, my Lord Greg, you *didn't know* your major? Just go away. Go, go and graduate fast. They may take it back if they find this out."

Hey, I didn't know. It's easy to miss some things occasionally. Pam told me not to tell anyone because they might find out they were dealing with an idiot. So maybe I had no earthly idea what I was majoring in. Is that a crime? I was taking courses to complete my college education and getting excellent grades. Isn't that what you're supposed to do? But as my good wife says, "Typical Greg."

21

TRI-ART PRODUCTIONS

My friend, Bill Townsend, and I put together a little recording studio in the basement of a duplex in which Pam and I were living. The studio in my basement wasn't much more than a little mixing box, a two-track recorder, and a limited microphone collection including two Electro-Voice 6-35 A's and a Sennheiser condenser. I learned as much as I could from an old gentleman in town who was interested in electronics and another man who had made some amateur recordings. It was all so fascinating to me. I spent hours listening to any microphone I could get my hands on, checking out various speakers, learning how cable connections altered sound, and learning how the signal path from microphone to the recording console worked. It was first grade stuff in the recording world and I was determined to learn. What with learning about the basic function of pre-amps, transformers, EQ, compression, limiting, and how to identify frequency ranges in the sonic spectrum, I was in seventh heaven. This is definitely where my obsessive-compulsive nature was a great advantage.

We named the studio Tri-Art Recording. I spent many fruitful preparatory years learning recording techniques, mixing, editing, microphone placement, using reverb, equalization, compression, and what microphones to use. I was constantly reading trade magazines.

The studio grew from a two-track, eight, sixteen, and finally a twenty four-track facility. We began recording local and regional artists using local musicians and high school kids, which was a great learning opportunity for us all. I played a lot of piano, bass, and cello in those days.

Bill graduated a year ahead of me in high school. He owned a laundry and was a pilot with a strong background in electronics. Recording was as exciting to him as it was to me and we hit it off immediately. He understood how to deal with creative types and was so patient and kind to me. We jumped into recording with both feet and it was an amazing time of exploring, education, and fulfillment for us. He definitely had business moxie and I never had to worry about that. It was a partnership that was loving and replete with trust. When we sold the business years later, it was a most pleasant ending. We remain friends to this day and when I'm in Bismarck, he and his beautiful wife, Alva, along with their children are on my must-see list.

Early on we recorded little school ensembles and then tried our hand at commercial jingles. We were always flying by the seat of our pants, and as I think back it was almost crazy. We only had a two-track recorder at that time. When we recorded we had to record on one track, then add another part and mix it to the opposite track and so on and so forth. What were we thinking?

On one occasion, executives from a local bank came over to my home so they could hear their new jingle. We nervously played our work and there were nods of approval. One of the gentlemen fancied himself as a musician and asked if he could have us raise the level of the singer.

Well, here was our problem. This was a final mix that could not be altered unless we started over again. I was at a total loss as to how we could respond, but just then, Bill reached over to the little mixer and raised one fader. The man who had the request gave us the A-OK thumbs up. What he didn't know was that the fader wasn't connected whatsoever to our mix. Nothing changed volume wise, but the visual of moving the fader up convinced the listener that something had changed. This was a trick I used many times later in my career when dealing with overzealous record execs and artist managers.

One of the most famous artists that recorded there was John Denver. John was on tour and had a concert in Bismarck. He was also in the process of finishing his album "Annie's Song." He had one more song to record and not enough time to get back to Los Angeles to make his deadline. We received a call from his manager asking what kind of equipment we had, and on hearing our studio configuration, booked the date. John came over to the studio which was now in Bill's basement. This set-up was a much more sophisticated environment than my basement. Mickey Crofford was the engineer they flew in from Los Angeles to record the song. You can look at the studio credits for that album and they read, "All songs recorded at RCA Recording Capital of the World, Los Angeles, except "The Music Is You" recorded at Tri-Art Productions, Bismarck, North Dakota."

With a recording studio in place I was able to experiment creatively with jingles and custom recordings. I had a strong desire to find new opportunities to get with people who were much better musicians than me. It was the beginning of moving away from the safety of the musical environment in which I was comfortable and actively seeking out more diverse and challenging opportunities.

I left my teaching job and for the next two years I worked one on one with kids from my church as a youth director. When I was teaching I noticed that there were a lot of troubled kids and it saddened my spirit. I went to my church and asked them to hire me so I could reach out to these precious students. They agreed and hired me. I told them I would not be starting any special programs, but I wanted to concentrate on building up the youth choir. I knew this was a great connecting point for kids at that time.

So began my life of talking to kids at schools, involving them in any musical projects in which I was working, and simply being a friend to many of them who were desperately lonely. I can't tell you why I quit teaching to do this, but somehow, somewhere deep in me I knew I needed to move out of my safety zone and begin a new season in my life. There was no big voice from God . . . but I knew He was doing the tugging.

I had freedom to work in any school, because I had worked with the teachers, administration, and support staff. It was an extremely fulfilling time and I was granted unusual favor. My friend, Ron Keller, began a Young Life chapter at that time and we worked closely together. These were days of counseling, youth choirs, and enlightenment to a genre born out of the Jesus Movement called contemporary Christian music. I was voracious in studying every album I could find. I sat at my office at the First United Methodist Church listening to Phil Keaggy's "What A Day." Andrae Crouch's "This Is Another Day." and the orchestrations of Ronn Huff of a musical by Bill and Gloria Gaither entitled "Alleluia."

I ordered the orchestrations to this musical and studied the score. I started calling people who worked on these records and through these contacts began to write the piano vocal books for artists like "2nd Chapter of Acts," "Keith Green," and others. This was the beginning of the end of my time in North Dakota. When I completed two years at my church, eight other congregations hired youth directors for their churches. I was now ready for a new season in my life, but it was a very difficult thing to say goodbye to what had been. The leaving never really left me, but God was near.

I will always love Bismarck, North Dakota, my hometown. I have boundless appreciation for the many gifted people who taught me (aware or unaware), guided, and extended so many countless and rich opportunities; but most of all, loved the frenetic little boy who lived on Shirley Street. A life-long tapestry of friends and memories is woven in my heart, ever reminding me of my ineradicable connection to that city and her people. It will always remain the center of my sense of place in this temporary world.

22

LEAVING

Ashes are often the most fertile ground for successful dreams.

I'd spent twenty-nine years in Bismarck, gone through the entire public school system, Bismarck Junior College, and graduated from the University of Mary (then Mary College). I taught in the grade schools and at Bismarck High School. I'd served as a youth director at First United Methodist Church, co-owned a recording studio, served in the Army Reserve for six years, directed three church choir programs in the Lutheran, Nazarene, and United Methodist churches, organized several performing groups, wrote jingles, and produced records. I knew that I was at a crossroads of my life. Would I stay here where I felt a sense of safety, acceptance, and security? Really can't say that I had processed all that I was feeling, but something in me said move on. Not knowing what that meant, there were a series of events that began to answer the question for me.

I had recorded an album for a songwriter/artist from South Dakota named Phill McHugh. That recording was submitted to Sparrow Records and picked up by Lamb and Lion Records, which was distributed by Sparrow Records at the time. We recorded the album at Tri-Art Productions. The orchestra was recorded at Pine Brook Studios in Indiana. It was really my first serious venture into producing, arranging, and conducting an orchestral score played by studio professionals.

I was scared to death. I walked into the studio and came face to face with my fears. When I began to conduct and hear what I'd written, such relief came over me. I was home in a sense. This was the beginning of my professional studio life, and a work for which I was born. The sessions went very well and I began to see the benefit of going after the unknown. Of course I had no idea what I was doing, and it was glaringly obvious to me that this favor I was being afforded was not anything remotely of my own doing.

I knew that my heart was in recording and if I were going to have an opportunity to arrange, I would have to start a record company to fulfill that need. I met with four businessmen from Bismarck and each of us invested $15,000.00 in this new recording entity called Spirit Records. In January of 1978 I began calling Billy Ray Hearn, the head of Sparrow Records. "Is Mr. Hearn in? This is Greg Nelson calling." Jackie, his receptionist replied, "I know who this is, I've given him your messages and I can't promise anything right now." "Okay, thank-you, Jackie."

So the conversation repeated itself for days, then weeks. I called every day trying to get his attention, and after a month of his assistant putting me off, he finally took my call. Billy Ray was aware that I had produced the Phill McHugh record. I told him I had a record company and he asked me how many artists I had. I told him I didn't have any artists and that's why I needed his help.

Within two weeks he came to Bismarck and we began discussions about a potential distribution arrangement between Sparrow and Spirit. I'd been writing piano/vocal books for Second Chapter of Acts and other Sparrow artists that were sub contracted to me by a musical composer/orchestrator named Phil Perkins in Texas.

It was this fact that led Billy Ray to ask me if I knew anything about publishing, and without a pause I said I did. (Of course, I didn't have a clue what a publisher did.) He then asked me if I would be interested in becoming his director of publishing, which would also allow me to be closer to the day-to-day operations of the record company. Immediately after I got off our phone call, I started calling everyone I could to find out what publishers did. Actually Spirit became a production company for Sparrow.

Pam and I had discussed the possibility of moving, but she told me that the only two places where she would not want to move would be New York or Los Angeles. We moved to Los Angeles in late spring of 1978. I moved a month prior to Pam and Sarah coming out. During that time, a wonderful musician friend of mine, Al Perkins, invited me to stay with him at his home on Lemp Avenue in North Hollywood. I met Al and John Michael Talbot when they came to North Dakota to play on a record I was producing. Artist agent, Ray Nenow, with whom we all had various business relationships, introduced all three of us.

Al Perkins, a well-known steel and guitar player, was a member of "Manassas" and "The Flying Burrito Brothers." His playing credits included Bob Dylan, Crosby, Stills and Nash, Roger McGuinn, James Taylor, Richie Furay, Chris Hillman, "The Nash Ramblers" with Emmy Lou Harris and later Garth Brooks. It was a high learning curve for me to be in the presence of some of these artists when they occasionally hung out with Al. Al was unbelievably gracious to me and hired me to write string charts for some of the artists with whom he worked. My time in Los Angeles was like taking a master's course in songwriting and production.

For the next two years I began a very intense study of the craft of songwriting, publishing agreements, approaches to mixing, selecting musicians, album flow, and mastering. I went to session after session, met with scores of songwriters and listened, listened, listened. I began to understand the corporate personalities of the various record companies and who the decision makers in the different areas of each company were.

I realized that I did not have the proclivity as a record company owner. I was so severely right brained that I really didn't have the slightest need for the left side of my head at all. I discovered much about the areas of creativity where I could blossom, and with the record company not doing as well as I hoped, I eventually sold it. We lost our shirts, and the investors who had trusted my judgment were let down.

This began a very dark period for me and I questioned why I had made the move to Los Angeles. They say what doesn't kill you makes you stronger. Through a difficult emotional process I began being resurrected from the ashes. I looked to what could be, taking to heart what I had learned. I realized I was not a process person and needed help in that area. I had to find people who could help me be the creative that I knew was my strength.

In the spring of 1980 I was given an opportunity to do two string arrangements in Nashville and flew there to record them. When I arrived, I found out that one of the projects had been put on hold and I was left with only one arrangement to record. This was a real low point financially. I was helpless to control what was happening, and again, prayed another prayer of desperation. Something told me I needed to sit tight. It was at this point in my life that I truly began to understand that prayer was powerful.

Why was I always waiting to pray in desperate times when I could be praying gratefully in a continuum? I found that as my faith was being refined through the fire of difficult circumstances, I was growing spiritually.

I sent what I had earned to Pam and Sarah in Los Angeles, and told Pam that I had a good feeling about finding work in Nashville. So for the next three months, I slept on the floor of my artist agent friend, Ray Nenow.

Ray was a booking agent/artist manager/record aficionado whom I had met years earlier when I still lived in Bismarck. Ray was a hippie who had seen the horrors of Viet Nam and loved rock-n-roll, while I was pretty vanilla and loved classical music. If I were listening to classical music in the car, he would tell me that it gave him a headache. We were the odd couple for sure. We both brought something to the table and our relationship was one of admiration and love.

Every day I went to record company offices and tried to talk to the executives and A&R (Artist and Repertoire) people, but to no avail. One of the best pieces of advice I got was from a musician who told me that the owner may be the head, but the assistants and secretaries are the neck that turns everything. Remembering that, I began spending hours and days talking to receptionists and meeting with assistants.

Finally, at the beginning of the third month, through the influence of one of these assistants, I got a little job remixing some old masters for one of the record companies, and resulted in me gaining favor with the label head, Bob MacKenzie. He gave me another job to produce a record called "Touch of the Master's Hand" on Wayne Watson, who would become one of the premier artists in our industry.

I spent a month and recorded the record for some small amount and sent that badly needed money home to my girls in Los Angeles. After a few days I was pretty much broke. I vividly remember my agent friend, Ray, and me presenting Wayne's project to the label head. I was excited to play it for him, but my excitement was short lived when he told me he wanted some of it remixed. The problem was the budget funds were depleted and I didn't have enough money to pay a studio and engineer to do any remixing.

I was dejected as I got into the car with Ray on that overcast summer day. He said, "Let's get something to eat," and I burst out crying. I turned to him, "Man, Ray, I'm broke, I don't have a penny in my pocket. He put his big old hippie arm around me and said, "I got you man; we'll figure something out. You'll see."

That night I prayed probably the most rambling cathartic prayer of my life. I was powerless to turn my life in any direction. I knew I could do good things if I just got the chance before the old economic train rolled over me. I went to bed relieved in a way, still with some heaviness, but not in the same way as before.

The following Tuesday Ray got off a call and said, "Greg, I just talked to Joe English and he wants to come to Nashville to record a gospel album." Ray's words to me were excited and it had been a long time since I had any sense of excitement except in the form of anxiety. Joe was the drummer for Paul McCartney and "Wings" and Ray was Joe English's agent. Ray talked to the record label interested in Joe and within a day he had secured a deal. Ray also made a condition of the deal that I would produce. I was dumbstruck. I still would have to find a way to pay bills in California and enough for me to eat because the album was a few months off.

Ray took me to Joe Moscheo. Joe was an executive at BMI and had been Elvis Presley's pianist. An unbelievable musician in his own right, Joe was a kid from Albany, New York, the son of Italian parents. His dad was a bi-lingual preacher at the Italian Christian Church.

Joe's father gave him piano lessons so he could play in church, but Joe loved rock and roll and never did play in his church. I met with Joe and He asked me how many songs I had written that had been on major records. I told him that I didn't have any. He then asked me if I planned to be writing for that album and I told him I was sure going to try. He called me "Dakota" and said, "Well, Dakota, I'll see what I can do." Ray and Joe spoke briefly and we left. I didn't really hold out much hope. How could I? I had no songwriter credentials at all.

That Thursday, Ray got a call from Joe and he wanted to see us. We got to his office and he said, "Well, Dakota, are you going to do me good here? I've checked you out and we think we'd like to help you." I couldn't believe it! He handed me an envelope and I was so excited that I gave him the biggest hug that Italian had ever received. Too nervous to open it, I waited till we got in the car to see how much it was. *If only I could get 500 dollars*, I thought, *I could send $450 to Pam and keep just enough to eat sparingly until the project or something else came through.* "Well, open it," Ray said. I opened it and was still afraid to see the number, so he grabbed it and looked at it. A big smile came over his face and he said, "You're not going to believe this," and he started laughing. At that point I didn't know what to think and I took it and there I saw a check for 10,000 dollars. Ray was right, I couldn't believe it.

It was at this time that the floodgates to my career opened. The next week, Randy Cox approached me and said he was starting Meadowgreen Music, a Christian publishing arm of the powerhouse publisher, Tree International. His writers included Michael W. Smith, Rich Mullins, Gary Chapman, Bev Darnall, Nan Gurley, Billy Sprague and Jim Weber among others. Randy asked if I would be interested in signing with him. Meadowgreen would put me on a weekly retainer and finance all song demos for me as an advance against royalties.

I experienced one blessing after another, and answers to my desperate prayers came rolling at me like a speeding train. I couldn't figure out why they were so interested in me, and still don't understand it really. With no songs and little legitimacy as a producer, I can only reckon that God had to be the one doing the promoting.

I needed to move my family to Nashville and tried to think of a way to have them come. So, I approached Bob MacKenzie, who I would be working with on the Joe English project. I timidly asked him for an advance to help me move Pam and Sarah from Los Angeles. In this meeting he abruptly told me, "I am not responsible for your problems," and that pretty much was the essence of my meeting and request. However, the following day his assistant called me and said that Bob was moving Pam and Sarah per my request and that it was to be a gift to me and not an advance. (The cost was a little over 3,000 dollars.)

Ray Nenow also helped me out of the Wayne Watson remix issue. He told me to wait a couple days and have Scott Hendricks, the engineer, just brighten and compress the mix a little, but not remix. He knew that Bob was mercurial in mood, and we should meet in the morning when he was fresh rather than in the afternoon. We did just that, and when we played him the album the second time, he turned and gave us a thumbs up. Ray just smiled at me. He knew people and I gleaned so much from him about temperament and corporate disposition.

Joe Moscheo became one of my biggest champions from that time on. At award shows he'd stop me and say, "Hey, Dakota, you did real good there," or "Hey, Greg. You need anything? You know I'll take care of you." Well, I did my best on the Joe English record and it was listed by *Contemporary Christian Magazine* as one of the top ten Christian albums of the year.

Ray continued to look out for me like a big brother. Right after I finished the English record I was summoned to the Benson Company and asked by one of the A&R people if I might be interested in a little known artist at the time whose name was Sandi Patty. It was my intersection with her that allowed me to produce the sort of music that really was the sum total of my musical parts. My work with her gave me an instantaneous credibility in the industry and I remain grateful to her to this day.

Some years later, another company offered me a production/ publishing deal. In order for me to accept this offer, I had to be released from my publishing agreement with Meadowgreen Music because I was still under contract. It was Randy Cox who allowed me to leave Meadowgreen Music, enabling me to take advantage of this offer. He was an extremely smart businessman as well as creative. He knew that I would be the first to gravitate toward songs he pitched me for subsequent recordings. He could see "the forest for the trees." It was not just his savvy as a publisher, but his real concern for my well-being. That was the way things used to be done back in the day.

Make no mistake about it. Billy Ray Hearn was my greatest mentor. He took the time to teach, nurture, chasten, encourage and bring me into the industry at the very beginnings of Sparrow Records. From time to time I would meet him at Richland Country Club for lunch and we would talk about the state of the industry. We'd talk about what each of us was doing, what our old friends were up to and I was still picking up words of wisdom from this seasoned warrior. I always reminded him of one particular kindness he showed me.

After I had sold Spirit Records, I received a phone call from Sparrow that I owed some multi thousands of dollars for returns that had come in on product. This was not unusual, but was picked up by subsequent sales of new product. Because I sold the company, there was no new product. I found myself in debt to Billy Ray.

At this time I was in Nashville, sleeping on Ray Nenow's apartment floor while trying to forge my way into the industry as a producer. I immediately called Billy Ray and told him that I could only pay him fifty dollars a week at most, and I didn't really know how I was going to do that and keep my family afloat. I assured him that I would make good on my debt. Then Billy Ray said to me, "Greggor, I can tell you how we can work this out. You keep your eyes and ears out for new artists and keep me abreast of what is happening in Nashville because I'm bringing Sparrow to Nashville."

I told him I would be glad to do that for him and thanked him for his forbearance in settling the debt I owed. He said "I don't think you understand, if you can do this for me, that will settle the matter." I cried my eyes out over the phone. I knew what he was doing for me. He was forgiving the debt. I think that's why I fully understand the significance of Matthew 18:26-27 so well. "So the slave fell to the ground and prostrated himself before him, saying, 'Have patience with me and I will repay you everything.' And the lord of that slave felt compassion and released him and forgave him the debt."

Billy Ray taught me many things, but this to me was a defining lesson in mercy and one I have lived out to this day. I brought Steve Green and Steven Curtis Chapman to meet Billy Ray, and made good on my promise to him. These talented men would come to be two of the most respected artists our industry has ever known.

I never forgot what Joe Moscheo did for me in my beginnings and I never left BMI. Billy Ray, Joe, and Bob MacKenzie passed away some years later. The industry mourned their passing and celebrated their lives. Ray moved away to North Carolina, but we have an ongoing relationship as I do with Randy, who is still writing and championing songs in Nashville.

I wanted to let you see in this season of my life, what I saw . . . or often couldn't see, that God was near . . . as I held on oh so tightly to that runaway horse.

23

THE NASHVILLE YEARS

A fter living thirty years in Bismarck and another two plus years in Los Angeles, I finally settled into the city where I would most likely live the rest of my life. Nashville had become the main center for Contemporary Christian Music and it was a season of tremendous growth in the industry. There was great opportunity and freedom in these years when entrepreneurs ran record companies and artists had freedom to be themselves and not slaves to a pre-determined marketing scheme. These were the best years in this industry and few of my colleagues would argue any differently.

The Nashville music community was a creative buzz of record labels, recording studios, publishing houses, artist management, marketing, sales, and radio. There was great interest in refining sound with newly created equipment to enhance and facilitate the recording process. The digital world was just in its infancy and there, of course, was no Internet. Music Row was the most creative working environment of my entire life and a perfect match for my abilities and strengths.

My days were spent in in the studio, meeting with record companies, managers, artists, writers, and publishers. I did spend a lot of time trying to find or modify various pieces of gear that would help me enhance the sonic quality of my records.

The process of recording an album was a long and winding road. First came the approach of the record company to find out if I was available to work on a project, then meeting the artist and at some point their management. I usually would be aware of the artist to some degree, so I had to determine if I had the time to work with them, if the chemistry felt right, and if I thought they had something important to say. I certainly did pray about those with whom I was asked to produce. However, the criterion was certainly different in the early days.

I was on a panel of producers where we were asked what determined the artists we chose. There were some very heavy hitting producers on this panel. (I have no idea how I got on it; probably somebody canceled.) As they went down the row, these studio maestros waxed quite eloquently on their criterion and how it was established. When they got down to the boy from Bismarck, I tried to tell them my truth. The truth for me was that when I first started to produce I would gladly have worked with an organ grinder's monkey if they would pay me. If they couldn't pay, I would have done it for free just for the experience. It was only later when I was more established, that I would have the blessing of discerning the creative and spiritual vision of an artist.

I found out a lot about artists by asking them what they liked to read and what songwriters and songs moved them. When we went out to eat, I always let them talk and tell me about themselves. I didn't have to say anything, because out of the abundance of the heart, the mouth speaks. If they were enamored by their accomplishments, who they knew, and if they didn't ask one question about my family or myself; I had my answer.

I heard this question often from industry people, "Where are you taking this artist or that artist on this next album?" The fact of the matter was that I was never taking an artist anywhere. My role as producer was to join in their vision for artistry and be a servant to them and make that vision happen. I spent my whole life facilitating the vision of an artist and bringing his or her dreams to fruition.

A key role for me was finding songs that represented the heart of an artist. Some producers wanted to hear a sophisticated demo, but I had a process that worked well for me. I only wanted to hear a piano, vocal, or guitar vocal of any song that was pitched to me. When I received the demo from whomever, my project coordinator knew that I wanted to see the lyric first. The reason for this was that in my mind's eye, it didn't really matter what the music was if the lyric didn't evoke something substantial in me.

Holly or Cindy (project managers) would sit with me for hours and go through song after song. Each project could elicit hundreds of pitches and days of reading and listening. After a while, these song warriors (Holly and Cindy) would already have thinned out the songs for me before they would hand me something they thought might work. If it had not been for these women, I would have not gotten half the work done that I did. They were two angels.

God gave me two rich treasures in Cindy Wilt Colville and Holly Krig-Smith. They are directly responsible for any success that I ever enjoyed. I was a lost little puppy without their guidance and the strength to challenge my thinking. As I write, there are tears of gratefulness to them both. Cindy and I met at Lorenz Creative Services. Elwyn Raymer and Steve Lorenz understood my need for organization and were very wise to put us together. Our love of songs and the God we loved was the joy in our work.

When I lost my sight in 1988 after a three-week trip to South America (more on that a couple chapters from now), it was Cindy who read my letters and the Bible to me, drove me to every appointment, and loved on me like a sister.

When Cindy left for theatrical work in New York, I worried that I could never replace her. So began the search that would become a team effort. I sat in the great room of our home in Brentwood with my wife and daughter, Sarah. The three of us met with each person who applied for the work of production assistant. We went through interview after interview. It was always the same response from my girls. "I think there is someone better for you, Dad."

Then in walked Holly Krig-Smith and the room lit up. She was bright, artistic, confident, and experienced as well. Holly was meticulous with everything she managed. She could have worked for far more important people than me, but she was as loyal as she was brilliant.

When I was in the middle of multiple projects, the reality was that I often spent more time with these women than I did with Pam. With long hours in the studio or studios for days, my wife and children needed to know that I would be safe in these special individuals' care. Cindy and Holly were strong. I got my share of rebukes from each of them when they felt I was not properly taking care of business. I loved these women from the time we met. I will never be able to fully express my deepest gratitude for their caring, loving capable direction as well as their spiritual presence in my life. No amount of thank-you's would ever be enough.

Later, Cindy became a vice president of publishing at Word Entertainment, but now has gone on to better things, heavenly things. Holly is now heading an arts school program near Atlanta. Holly, her husband, Steve, children Madeline and Emma Smith, remain fast friends to this day.

The next step in the process was bringing songs to the artist I thought might work. The artists would then sift through these entries and say yes, no, or maybe. I was very fortunate to have been given great freedom by record companies, and was never closely micro managed like many others were in this regard. Bottom line, the artist determined what went on the record, but at times would defer to my sensibilities if I felt strongly about a particular song.

There were many, many meetings with artist, management, A&R people, and marketing people. Songs were put "on hold," meaning that the publisher would not pitch these songs to anyone else unless the hold on the song was removed.

Producers were expected to: hire the studios, mastering houses, engineers, track musicians, background singers, choral contractors, arrangers, orchestrators, copyists, gear rental, cartage, orchestra contractors, book hotels, secure visas, and turn in finished album credits with final cd and accompaniment mixes. I would sit down with Holly or Cindy and go through the musicians I wanted on particular projects. These would change with each artist and it was essential to be aware of the player's temperament and drummer/bass combinations. In short, knowing which players could deliver the right sensibility for whatever genre in which I was working. I had learned many things during my time in Los Angeles along with lessons learned in the formative stages of my career in Bismarck. It made my transition in Nashville much easier.

One of the funniest/stupidest moves I made in hiring was when I was working on my first Larnelle Harris record and wanted to establish a real "black gospel" feel. I associated R&B with anything soulful, so I assumed that R&B players would naturally be able to play black gospel. I proceeded to hire a great section with Randy McCormick on piano from the Muscle Shoals hit section, Larry Byrom on guitar (Steppenwolf), James Stroud (Marshall Tucker) and Dave Hungate, bassist with Toto who had just moved from LA to Nashville. After the first few run throughs, it didn't take long for me to understand that the wide sweeping style of black gospel styled piano with constantly altered chord changes was a far cry from a "sit down" R&B groove. I had done Randy McCormick a grave injustice, and after but a few valiant efforts on his behalf, I was at least smart enough to shut the session down.

The players walked into the room all knowing the issue. I told them that I had made a greenhorn mistake. I told them I was embarrassed and they could just turn in their union cards and I would pay them for the day. At this, they all started to chuckle and patted me on the back telling me not to worry about the money. David Hungate smiled and said, "I've never been fired from a gig before. This is a first." James said, "Me either." Come to find out, none of them had ever been fired from a session. I had administered their first work release. (I paid them for a lesson you can't find in books.)

If you see this only as my flawed thinking, for me there was deeper meaning. These players' tenderness and gentleness toward me in this situation is the stuff of what created the inextricable bond we felt in the comings and goings in each of our lives on Music Row. People really cared about each other and were very protective of one another. That love and camaraderie was the fuel for unbelievable emotion in the music and lyrics emanating from Nashville. We were family.

Studio work could be a blitzkrieg or like wading in molasses. Generally, I would arrive at the studio at 9:30 in the morning to get ready for my first session. My day was usually the same while recording. Sessions were in three-hour segments. 10:00 in the morning until 1:00 with an hour break for lunch, then 2:00 until 5:00 and an hour break for dinner, then 6:00 till 9:00. Many nights after the musicians left, we might do rough mixes to hear what we had just done or comp vocals. ("Comp" means taking the best performance from a number of takes and combining them into a working or final vocal.) These late night sessions could go on sometimes into the middle of the night, and many times I could hear birds chirping as I left the studio.

Generally, I would be in the middle of two or even three projects at the same time. It was not unusual to work these hours steadily six days a week for up to three months at a time with little rest in between. Don't get me wrong, I loved what I was doing and with my obsessive-compulsive nature, I did not view it as work. I'd lie in bed at night; turn to Pam and say, "I can't believe they're paying me to do this." May I never take for granted this blessing of being able to do the very thing I love.

There were always inner struggles for me. Earlier in my career I was content in my own small musical sphere. The music I was producing was inspirational. It had its own musical personality and audiences had a certain musical expectation. The money was great and work was constant.

But as time went on this became debilitating to me because I found myself repeating the same thing over and over. Fulfilling expectations, but feeling the restraint to creatively move forward. What ensued were feelings of restlessness and a struggle to evolve.

My dilemma was either to continue enjoying commercial success or follow my own artistic yearning and dreams. Here was the rub. It wasn't just about me. What about the artist? It was their record and reputation, not mine. What about my family and their welfare? It's not just my risk, but risking my family's well-being. It was a constant war.

The contemporary Christian market place of magazines and radio charting leaned generally toward a "hipper" Christian audience of music lovers. Inspirational music was viewed as vanilla and saccharine. The term I heard a lot was "Republican pop."

Interestingly, the inspirational artists were a powerhouse of record sales as well as a print publishing and artist-track selling bonanza. I struggled with not being the hipster, but eventually came to a genuine gratefulness for the sum total of parts that God had given me.

There were many people involved in a major recording session and a litany of tasks. The first job was to find an available studio, engineer, and schedule players or singers. When drums were being used, we would arrange with the studio to have them brought in the night before so the drumheads could settle into the room. The piano needed to be tuned before each day's sessions and it was also important to have fresh fruit, drinks, and snacks for the players. Next was to arrange with the cartage people to have my speakers, amplifiers, and racks of pre-amps, compressors, EQ, microphones, or any other rented outboard gear delivered.

It was common to be working in and out of multiple studios in one day so I had duplicate speakers and amplifiers in order to have a continuum of audio perspective. In other words, I was relying on the same speaker/amp reference from studio to studio, rather than trying to understand the speaker personality traits in each studio set up. All of this gear was really important and most all of it had been modified in some way. It wasn't just about one electronic element alone, but the unique combination of pieces in the audio arsenal. I had many pre-amps that had switchable transformers, which brought even more nuance to the sound color. I loved vintage tube microphones, EQ's, and compressor/limiters that were the pallet of sound paint bringing a recording to an exquisite vibrancy. There were virtually hundreds of combinations to find what would sound the best to my ears for any singer, instrument, or musician. We would spend hours searching for just the right sound in the sound chain, and continually experimented with microphone placement.

For orchestral recording in London or Los Angeles, engineers would set up a decca tree of three microphones high above the front of the orchestra. This configuration worked best in huge studios, redone churches, or sound stage recording venues. As the orchestra would run down the music, the engineer mixed the sound using only those three microphones, and what you heard was what you got. There may have been a limited amount of close miking, but really there was little you could do to effectively rebalance the levels later. Recording these sessions was heart pounding and your ears had to be at their very best.

Orchestra sessions could be sabotaged by the shoddy copy work of a copyist who prepared the orchestral score. Mistakes meant wasting time to discover and correct. Thankfully I was fortunate to have some of the best of this talent available. When you were on the floor with anywhere from thirty to ninety players in a session, multi-thousands of dollars were spent in one three-hour session. There was a tremendous amount of pressure to move quickly, smartly, and achieve a performance as close to perfection as possible. Wise decision-making as to what take would be accepted and what little mistakes in an overall performance would be left for sake of the overall feel were critical.

The sum total of my experiences all came into play. Sitting in front of you in London, Los Angeles, Nashville, and New York studios were the finest recording musicians in the world. We played in studios like Abbey Road, Air, Phoenix, RCA, Ocean Way, and countless other orchestral sound stages throughout my career.

Record companies wanted results for the hundreds of thousands of dollars being spent on their artists for production, marketing, distribution, radio, publicity, and artist advances. Your career hung in the balance on the success of your last record. I think I did not allow myself to think about what might be, but on what was directly in front of me at the time. One bite out of the elephant each day, and with all the care and attention I could bring to each moment in the studio.

Getting a vocal from a great artist is such a mix of the condition of their voice, time of day, room temperature, allergy season, how rested they are, their immediate emotional state, and a musically intuitive engineer. The best possible scenario is just having the engineer, the producer, and the artist in the process. In the actual session the goal is to get the best possible vocal and there are various approaches to this. Every producer works differently with his or her artist.

Through the initial stages of recording a vocal you quickly come upon a comfortable mojo with each artist. Initially, a song might take a little longer for the singer to "find their voice" but when that is achieved things move quickly. If a singer was having continual problems with a song, nine times out of ten it would be due to a wrong key selection or a tempo issue. I liked to let the singer get to a point where they felt good about a few takes. Then we'd let them rest while the engineer and I did a quick comp, and if necessary we could go back and fix what we thought might be better. One thing I wish I would have had was access to a great vocal coach. They are so capable of making something quite lackluster into something fabulous. Just a few tips and vocal exercises can make a tremendous difference to even the best of artists.

When an artist is in the studio singing, they relate to their performance with moments of a fragile ambiguity or bursts of a commanding assuredness. The producer's job is always to encourage and know when to offer suggestions or remain silent. I had to be careful because my obsessiveness could be frustrating not only to the artist, but to the engineer as well. That was one of my most difficult issues in the studio.

I loved working with strong artists because they knew what they wanted. The whole process of making a recording involves the creative overlap between artist, musicians, engineer, producer, and sometimes songwriter or orchestrators. The power of a great recording comes from the vision of the artist and the ability of the creative forces involved to bring that vision to fruition. I can recall many times when a contributor on a session would say something that sparked a direction for a song that would take the song from okay to great.

Egos had to be checked in at the door because so much could be missed with the cancer of narcissism. It doesn't take long to find those with whom you enjoy working. The greatest players were the best team players. Their talent spoke for itself. I have found these musicians to be some of the kindest, most curious, and willing to make sure that you got exactly what you needed from them on every session. They have been a wonderful source of joy and education.

I'd like to add that none of this work goes anywhere without the efforts of management, record company leadership, a great creative marketing staff, radio promotion, sales force, designers, and media among others. The industry was so fortunate to have *Contemporary Christian Magazine* and its great staff headed by John Styll. Sometimes the creative element takes these contributors lightly. The fact is that no one person can take too much credit. We have all been in this together and for me it has been a great run.

I want to give my great thanks to the finest engineers with whom I worked. I spent the lion's share of my time in the studio with these men who were artists in their own right. I will never forget their persistence in bringing about the best possible sonic performances while enabling a fertile creative environment for artists, musicians, and singers. The help of the various second engineers and interns in all the studios was also critical. There was always a tremendous creative overlap of producer, engineer, musician, and artist. It was never about one person. My success is the direct result of the amazing work by all of these individuals. We did it together.

I am overwhelmed with gratefulness to the music community that enabled me to enjoy such a wonderful career. I've met a lot of amazing people in the music business. Those who, like me, were there because they loved music, the messages in the music, not to mention the camaraderie of the artists, musicians, singers, engineers, songwriters, publishers, song pluggers, studio crews, cartage guys, production assistants, arrangers, orchestrators, copyists, record executives, and managers.

Money and fame never drove most of these people. The only power they felt was the impact of the music in their heart as they were making it. Ray Charles said it best. "I was born with the music inside me. Music was one of my parts. Like my ribs, my kidney, my liver, my heart. Like my blood. It was a force already within me when I arrived on the scene. It was a necessity for me—like food or water." In another interview he stated, "I never wanted to be famous. I just wanted to be great." Oh sure, I've met leaders and individuals who at the expense of others had a regrettable need and an insatiable thirst for significance, but they were few and far between. It was a very good season in music.

To Sparrow, Word Entertainment, Warner-Atlantic, Benson, Brentwood Records, Visual Bible (David Seibert and Dan Johnson), Amplified Administration, The Copyright Company, and Lifeway. I cannot express my gratitude adequately enough for all your help, opportunity, and guidance along the way.

It was always invigorating for me to be around the prodigious members of the music community. People operating at this level were unbelievably gracious and helpful and there was no pretense. They were outstanding in their performance, but equally extraordinary human beings. They would go out of their way to help.

I felt many times that musicians/singers etc. were sometimes taken for granted because people were so used to having this high level of musical prowess. I was always in absolute awe. This experience for me clearly brought into focus that these were men and women in possession of a huge measure of a God-given gift. Not only do they have this talent, but spend extensive, tedious, and disciplined hours honing it through personal diligent practice.

Music community, I bow to you, albeit figuratively, and want you to know that I'm humbled to have been fortunate enough to benefit from your talent and kindness. Very few days pass for me that I don't have this come to mind. Thank you, with everything that's in me.

Somehow I knew that I had been groomed all my life for such a time as this. It was a spiritual experience to me. Whenever I stood on the studio floor as the musicians were singing or playing, the sound rose up around and through me, and I was transported to unexplainable beauty. The life work of all these musicians and the passion emanating from each individual literally flowed into me as I stood there. It was if God was singing, and the wonder of those moments remain with me to this day.

24

ARTISTS AND STUDIO LIFE

Artists are a special breed. To me, there are many singers who have amazing voices, but being an artist isn't just about having a great voice. It is more about a distinctive manner of communication. They have what I call the "it" factor or *je ne sais pas ce que*. Great artists have charisma and style. The word "style" by its own description means "limitations." In that sense they are truly unique. There are many singers who sing "like" other singers, but that is not artistry. I would not enjoy the life singers have to lead traveling on buses and having to endure airports. It is an exciting life, but very difficult indeed. I have the greatest respect for these who are gifted, disciplined, perseverant, and devoted to their audience.

A producer's job is to create a safe place for the artist, one of love and respect. Technical skill is important, but there is much more in production. The recording process must allow the artist to go to this place of vulnerability, knowing that sometimes risk involves embarrassment or failure, but having the assurance that there is no judgment in the control room. The whole process is one of tremendous intimacy. The producer brings a point of view or reference for an artist. It is not an easy job. There are times when you have to let an artist know that the performance is just not there, so you try and let them down easy by saying things like, "That was perfect; let's do one more."

You are constantly going with your musical "gut," and this is where your gift becomes apparent. Any artist or producer can make sounds, but not everyone can make music.

We were recording Sandi Patty at Pine Brook Recording Studios in Alexandria, Indiana. Her office would send their bus to Nashville to pick up the engineer and me to record her vocals in Indiana where Sandi lived. She was eight months pregnant with twins and in order to give her some measure of comfort we had to rest her poor tummy on a stool while she sang. We couldn't believe she could even utter a sound in her motherly condition, but she sang like a bird. Her stamina was incredible, but she was always hot and wanted the air conditioning at the lowest temperature possible. Going for a "take" on one song, she nailed the vocal and came happily into the studio. As soon as she walked in, she said, "Is it warm in here or is it just me?" Joe Neil, the engineer, and I were sitting in our chairs with parkas on and Joe was wearing ear muffs. She took one look at us and we all fell out laughing. We couldn't get another thing done that day.

This was an emotional time for her as well. Joe and I would come to the studio at noon and wait for Sandi to arrive. Sometimes we would wait for an hour or two, but we could tell as soon as she walked into the control room, if we were actually going to do any recording that day. Our cue would be how much time it took from the time she walked in with a big smile to the time there were tears in her eyes. There were days when singing was just too much for all that was going on in her life. We'd just look at each other and say "nope" or ask each other what movie was playing in Muncie.

Those were pressurized days for this woman because her amazing voice was responsible for delivering great performances before packed houses with thousands in attendance, the wellbeing of a record company, print publishing, her management, concert promoters, musicians, and staff, not to mention the health of twins yet to be born. I was aware of this responsibility. I knew it wasn't just about not recording for one or two days, but about carrying a burden so daunting that I don't really quite understand how she managed to handle it all. I was always amazed at the level of professionalism and musicianship of the artists with whom I worked.

The recording of Sandi Patty's *More Than Wonderful* album was a tense time for me. It was the second album on which she and I worked together. This was before the days of auto tune and digitally being able to manipulate words and phrases on a vocal. Editing tape was done with a razor blade and sometimes we used as many as three or four people to help us move faders when we mixed.

On this particular record I was charged with producing a live record in the studio. This meant that all of the rhythm, full orchestra, background singers, and the artists had to be captured in one take. Our engineer was Bob Clark, one of the finest engineers in Christian music. Performing this daunting task could not really have been executed as quickly and efficiently by anyone else at that point in our history. He was a stickler for checking cables, microphone selection, punch locations, and he had a team of second engineers running around constantly rechecking at every possible opportunity.

I don't want to overstate this, but having the best possible microphone for an artist was essential. To me every piece of equipment and every action in the studio bows to the artist. The microphone is the beginning of the process. The vocalist and microphone are very special allies. The microphone takes the physical sound waves of the acoustical event and transfers them into a whole other medium. The pre-amps, EQ, transformers, and compression coif the sound, thus taking a musical action and turning it into a viscerally artful communication.

So then came the day of the recording. David Clydesdale, another giant in our industry, wrote and conducted all of the charts on this record and was as detailed, seasoned, and focused as any conductor you could hope to have. We had been painstaking in the selection of the songs and spent weeks and months narrowing the list. We were as prepared as we possibly could be down to the refinement of the music copyist work.

I remember Larnelle Harris walking into the studio at the exact moment we were to begin. Sandi was waiting for him in the small vocal booth, they greeted one another and both were smiling as they adjusted their headphones. Having done this many times before, they knew it was "go" time.

The room was electric and there was great unspoken drama bubbling up in the room and high anxiety on my part. In the recording business, a producer is only as good as his last record, and for me it was like rolling the dice. I knew what Sandi and Larnelle were capable of vocally, and it was my challenge not to miss those fleeting moments when they were peaking in the theatre of the song. We tweaked each section of the orchestra, rhythm, singers, and ran the song down once to see where we needed to ride the vocal levels.

Even on the run down the recording light was always on because in many instances with singers and musicians operating at such an incredible level, it was always possible that we might get a performance on the very first sight-reading that could not be bettered with any subsequent attempt.

The recording began. Bob Clark came on the headphone system and said, "We're rolling." The music began and the Spirit was moving. Everything for which I prayed on sleepless nights was coming to fruition. There is no way to describe what that emotion is in real time. I was tense, hopeful, inspired, grateful, and relieved all rolled into one. The orchestral track of Sandi Patty's performance of "More Than Wonderful" was recorded on the first take. We repaired one vocal line she sang with the orchestra and the entire album was recorded in two and a half days.

There was a project I was producing in New York— recording the American Boy Choir. My assistant had sent the music to them so they could familiarize themselves with the piece. We arrived at the studio early and we waited for them. Five minutes before the start time they filed into the studio in uniforms and lined up in front of the microphones where we had placed stands for their music. My librarian walked out and began placing the music in front of them. Very quickly, their conductor with whom I was conversing in the control room told me there is no need for music. They had memorized the entire piece and were ready to record immediately. We were done in about forty-five minutes and they marched out of the studio just as they had entered.

One of the funniest pranks ever pulled in the studio was by a producer friend of mine. He was working with a couple of well-known married artists whose little dog was yipping all the time they tried to work. This drove him crazy. So one day when the clients left for lunch, he went down to the nearby market and bought a Baby Ruth bar. He came back, took it out of the wrapper, and began molding it to look like a little "dog offering." He placed it strategically next to the console and waited for the clients to come back.

When they arrived it was business as usual and they begin to discuss doing the next take of a vocal. When the dog yipped again, my buddy pretended like he stumbled over something, looked down, and said, "What's that? Oh my goodness! Look!" and pointed to the "dropping" he had left earlier. The client's wife gasped as my friend picked it up and began to sniff it. At this point, everyone in the room was getting grossed out. Just like that, he popped it in his mouth and started chewing on it exclaiming, "Not bad." At this the woman grabbed her mouth and went running out of the room with her dog. However, her husband was almost rolling on the floor with laughter, fully understanding the point that was being made. Let's just say that was the last time the dog showed up for any session again.

I have recorded many albums with Steve Green over a thirty-year span. I serve as a board member of his ministry and have a great appreciation of his integrity. Steve is absolutely meticulous about the theological disposition of each and every word that he sings. In one instance he was reticent to sing a line in an oratorio that Bob Farrell and I had written called "Saviour." The line was from the section entitled "Rose of Sharon" in a reference to Jesus. It read, "This bloom so fair was taken before its time." We had written thinking that Jesus was only thirty-two when he was crucified. Steve, however, thought Jesus had not died prematurely, but exactly when God ordained it.

He was correct. Bob and I saw the wisdom of the change and we adjusted the lyric. Steve understood that many get their theology from a song lyric and he did not want to mislead with lyric that was inaccurate or unclear.

A little later I was reading my Bible and discovered that nothing is taken from God that He does not freely give. We had already mixed the record, so I went to the publisher of the choral book and had them overlay an asterisk that read "given." Now the entire phrase reads, "This bloom so fair was given in its prime."

Another favorite artist of mine was Scott Wesley Brown. We had so many fun times together because we both like to joke and pun back and forth. Occasionally, he would come up with little misnomers like the time he was speaking of the tympani when he said, "Greg, I think the 'tiffanys' are a little too loud." But my favorite was when he called me up after listening to the mastered recording on which we were working and wanted to encourage me about how good the record sounded. He told me, "phonically, this sounds amazing." He meant "sonically." We teased each other back and forth and continue to this day. I loved writing and recording with Scott.

Larnelle Harris is one of the most unique voices I have ever heard and I was more than honored to have him ask me to produce some of his recordings. He has an uncanny way to interpret a song. He can move seamlessly from a powerful stress point to a most sensitive and intimate moment, and all within the length of one phrase. This man knows how to tell a story. His beautiful instrument is an exquisite confluence of Pop, Soul, and Classical.

Getting a vocal from him was never complicated. He walked into the studio, delivered the goods, and left. Most people don't know this, but he is an excellent drummer. His soulful duets with Sandi Patty are legend and his rendition of Alan Moore's arrangement of "Amen" is a classic. Always anxious to get home, Larnelle is a family man with his precious wife, Mitzi, and their two children, Lonny and Teresa. His heart was never far from Kentucky. That was a great witness to me, and a reminder to keep the most important things . . . the most important.

Wayne Watson was the first artist that I worked with when I came to Nashville. Later in his career we reunited to work on two more recordings as well as a number of multiple artist projects. Working with Wayne was a pleasure for me to say the least. He is probably one of the most prolific songwriter/artists that our industry has ever seen and he is as thoughtful a man as he is kind. As we worked in the studio we enjoyed him sharing many memorable lines from "The Andy Griffith Show" and he kept us well humored.

I was fortunate to have worked with brilliant black gospel and theatrical artists like Richard Smallwood, Bebe and Cece Winans, Shirley Caesar, Jennifer Holiday, Mel Carter, South Africa's SDASA Singers and Florida Mass Choir. I can honestly say I was "taken to school" by each one of these gifted individuals. Looking back on my experiences has caused me to wonder why record companies used me to produce these prodigious black artists. It occurred to me that record executives in the companies with which I worked were white, and they tended to use producers operating in their own cultural sphere. I think that many times these artists would have been better served with black producers who were vested in the culture. I'm not trying to make any racially divisive statement here, but I'm just saying that I felt a little out of place at first. The Richard Smallwood Singers session was a good example of which I'm speaking.

Richard is a genius musician and songwriter. No one, and I mean no one, can more tend to a melody like he does. Each series of chord substitutions and harmonic progressions weaved by him are like a rare work of art. On my very first session with him, we had just finished a take of the first song of the day and I felt really good that we had gotten a nice "tight" track. Richard approached me, looked at me, rubbed his thumb and middle fingers together and said, "Greg, we need a little more grease on the track." It took me a few moments, but I realized what he was saying to me. What I had done was set up a click track for Richard and the band to follow. These were all the top white session players who played on many R&B/Gospel sessions.

Long story short, I was hamstringing Richard with a rigid metronomic click-track. It was what I usually did on tracking dates. He was telling me that I was removing any semblance of feel with the click track and it was impeding his ability to express the music the way he was feeling it. The fact of the matter was the singers sang best when they could respond to Richard in real time. So began my schooling from a masterful artist.

We quickly set up the singers in a booth so they could see Richard and everything was recorded together except the lead vocal. The result was obviously so much better than what I had tried to do. I think that I was also unconsciously bigoted when it came to hiring a black arranger or orchestrator. That was more a result of really not knowing any of these individuals because my tendency was to seek out arrangers and orchestrators from the circles in which I traveled. Black singers and session players were amazing to me and I could never have continued to have opportunities to produce without the likes of Tommy Sims, Jackie Street, Donna McElroy (Berkley College of Music professor), Vicki Hampton, Kim Fleming, and Bob Bailey just to name a few.

But it wasn't until I heard the group Take Six and got to spend real quality time with Mervyn Warren that I realized what I was missing. I heard his arrangements and I was floored. He operated his initial production work out of my office with Holly Krig-Smith helping him coordinate his productions. This enlightenment also spurred me on to seek out other creative minds I had never considered before. Mervyn was a Grammy winning producer and film score composer in his own right. Sorry for the cliché, but for me it has always been "live and learn."

I have found myself in the most incredible situations throughout my career. On one year-long project, I was flown to the Isle of Man multiple times and stayed at a castle on the isle. We ate meals at restaurants and pubs along the coast of the Irish Sea and got to watch the preparations for the Tourist Trophy Motorcycle Race. (The most deadly race in the world.) It was a fascinating view and experience. Later I was put up in London hotel rooms with my own butler, sitting only a table away from some of the most recognizable personalities in the world, and all the while feeling as George Gobel put it so well, "Like a brown pair of shoes with a black tuxedo." I just didn't fit in. Too much Midwest in me to ever change that I guess. After this particular project was over, I was given a week's vacation at the Ritz-Carlton with my family, along with twelve art pieces of Bunyan's "Pilgrim's Progress" that dated back to the late 1600's. It was a memorable year.

One of the goofiest things that ever happened to me in a studio, happened in London. I was recording the orchestra for two major projects, "Saviour" and "The New Young Messiah" in a one week period. This was with an eighty-piece symphony orchestra at CTS Studios, which was adjacent to Wembley Stadium. The first day we got set up, began getting sounds and rehearsing.

We broke at 1:00 for lunch, but I was still a little jet lagged from the flight and opted to stay in the control room to sleep during the break. Everyone went to lunch and a little later the second engineer came back up and asked me if I wanted anything to eat. I told him that I didn't and he followed up by asking me if I would like anything to drink. He reeled off a list of options, one of which was cider. Well, I love apple cider and so I told him that cider would be fine. A little later he came up with a tall glass of cider and I thanked him for his kindness. Well, I proceeded to drink down this cider, which tasted a little different than the cider I was used to, but it was pretty good. I finished it up and laid back down.

A little later the musicians and engineer came back and I sat up. Well, let me tell you, I got dizzy as a bee and something else was very apparent. I couldn't feel my lips.

This cider wasn't what I thought and I was already getting a headache and my stomach was churning. This was *powerful* cider and not like the cider I thought it was. I barely made it through the afternoon and was relegated to putting up a sign that said "KEEPER," informing the engineer that I liked the take. I was sicker than a dog.

For someone who drinks this would not be any problem whatsoever, but for this abstainer it was "factory shutdown" stuff. I don't drink that much cider of any kind anymore. *SHEESH!*

There are so many stories of gifted artists with whom I've worked. Thousands of hours were spent bringing their recordings to life, and it would take an entire book to recount stories of these people because each one is so disparate in the approach to artistry. The truth is that most artists only let you "in" just so far. They are an unusual brew and are left with little time in the course of family, the grind of the road, performances, interviews, outside obligations, preparations for concerts, writing, and the frenetic pace of the studio. Close friends require an investment of time, and generally that's not the kind of time a successful artist has.

At the center of all recording is the song. The songwriter slogan is, "It all begins with the song" and it was the songs that kept me working as a producer.

25

FROM THE HEART TO THE PAGE

Songwriting is one of the most wonderful gifts God ever gave me. I don't recall exactly how it all began, but the excitement of the process thrilled me. My days in writing rooms on Music Row were some of the most educational and freeing moments of my life.

To begin writing your first song is like skydiving for the first time. You're exhilarated, but in a swim of trepidation. Many times I'd write something I thought was brilliant, only to find myself saying after reviewing it some weeks later . . . "*What* was I thinking?" Undeterred, I kept writing because it was in my bones, my DNA, and it brought indescribable joy and satisfaction.

Songs emerge via all manner of moods, settings, and circumstance. Sometime they're called a treasure and compared to that of birthing a baby. But really, if you have children, you just can't make that kind of comparison. It's more a mystical birth, and I can only deduct that it is most certainly heavenly charity. I have no other way to surmise how a song comes to be.

I don't recall when I decided to sit down and write a song. I knew I loved words and certainly music. Cumbersome at first, I initially settled for the first thing that came to mind whether lyric or music. I thought that most everything that burst from my imagination was a little short of brilliant, only to discover later it was mind fodder at best. Shortly after attempts to write something of substance, I discovered I had mined the depths of my knowing and found I was in the shallow end of both notes and thoughts. Writing about questions no one was asking and introspection with little universal application kept sending me aimlessly to another clever dead-end. It was time to refill the tank, by listening, reading and observing.

So began my trek into the world of songwriting. There were a few complications for me on this road, the greatest being my inability to concentrate. It was very difficult to stay focused on anything. I was distracted easily. I learned to deal with it, but it was a challenge as I began to take songwriting seriously. As time went on, I discovered that I could hyper-focus, quickly analyze songs, and understand how they might serve particular artists. I knew beyond any shadow of a doubt this was God given, because this ability flew in the face of my attention deficit issues.

I began a relentless discipline of analyzing every song I listened to and voraciously studied all styles and genres of music. (My car and music room were strewn with a blur of records and cassettes.) My obsessive-compulsive nature was helpful in this cause, and learning came by listening to conversations, not so much by reading. Staying focused while reading a book was next to impossible for me. I loved poetry because it was written in short verses and it was easy for me to remember. I was enamored with each author's fascinating use of words.

Acting in high school and summer-theater was another way of learning about story lines. Songwriters create emotional story lines with music that serves the story. The relationship between words and music, called "prosody," has the music serving the lyric in the midst of the overall story line's prosodic landscape. As a cellist and conductor, I have played in countless musical productions. These experiences helped me develop an understanding of how to create tension and release lyrically, melodically, and harmonically.

Meter and rhythmic patterns were fascinating to me and comedians were a great source to teach the use of tempo for spinning a tale. After all, a story is paramount to a songsmith, a scriptwriter, or even a marketer. When pitching an idea, you have to convey your idea powerfully and succinctly. Though song lengths vary, you have on the average three-and-a-half minutes to tell your story.

I viewed a documentary Hitchcock/Truffaut, and was captivated by the discussion between filmmaker, Alfred Hitchcock, and French filmmaker/critic, François Truffaut. They spoke of three basic elements in filmmaking. The first element is film edits' behavior over time. The second is that film controls moments that are fast and slows them down. The third, that film takes moments, which are slow, and speeds them up. This is akin to what happens in a song. A songwriter is always editing the narrative to keep a clear, concise, and continuing account. My personal mantra is "fewer words, always fewer words."

Musical output is a combination of our overall culture—what we listen to, the period of history in which we were raised, our religious or non-religious background, the books we've read, the art we've experienced, our ethnicity, how the political conversations we heard as we grew up related to a world view, and so many other factors that all affect the musical and lyrical messages we create. In music as in all things, to grow you must risk. Growth requires creative curiosity, a measure of bravery, and being willing to fail. It is not difficult to spot a songwriter's "go to" tendencies. They manifest themselves by using the same song forms, lyrical phrases, rhythmic patterns, rhyming schemes, and redundant subject matter. Most every smithy has certain ways of approaching songs, but the great ones know how to make all things fresh with each new effort.

Every writer has his or her own personal style and manner. For example I'm not a prolific writer and it takes me a long time to birth and complete anything creative. The fact of the matter is that some writers don't like writing with me because I'm plodding in the process. I take too much time. But that's me.

The authenticity of a writer expressing what moves them has tremendous strength. Writers or artists are weakened when they chase after something, someone, some industry standard by just trying to fit in. Being true to one's own musical and lyrical instincts is a potent powerhouse, but being teachable is how we grow and learn. We are translators of sorts. We hear or see something and ingest it into our own creative psyche. What emanates from our pen is the "back translation" of what we saw and heard. It's our version of a style, sound, or story.

I have enjoyed having three main co-writers in my lifetime. They are Phill McHugh, Bob Farrell, and Paul Marino. This is not to ignore some writers with whom I have written some wonderful songs, but these three are the main writers in the three major seasons of my writing career. I have learned so much from these gentlemen, and could never have enjoyed the creative journey I've had without them. I remain indebted to each of them and for a lifetime I'll be grateful.

Industrial songwriters are used to setting up writing appointments, either morning, afternoon, or evenings. In that time period, the song is conceived and completed. Usually someone has an idea percolating and the writers go from there. I like to spend an afternoon or two just talking about a concept with whomever I am writing.

When I know if the idea is a hook, maybe a line in the song, or just the overall topic sentence, it is much easier for me to map out the song form. It's like a little three-minute movie. Verse one sets up the chorus, the second verse further develops the concept, then back to the chorus or central theme. If needed, we might insert a little two- or four-line bridge to vary the setup of the central chorus hook once more. Of course, this is only one song form I mention here. There are many different iterations of form. The Beatles for instance did the reverse of what I've just mentioned. They started out with the hooky refrain and used a bridge to create release, or if the opening refrain was more laid back, they used the bridge to create more tension. The character of this bridge is different from a bridge used in a verse chorus format and even more removed from a bridge section found in some extended worship songs. Those worship song bridges are entities unto themselves.

When the song form and rhythmic patterns are formed, the music comes very easily. Sometimes the musical hook or verse with a little lyric idea comes first. These are just basic forms, but there are many ways to put a song together. I advise young writers to write using basic rules and formats before they break those rules. There are writers who are so gifted that they have an immediate and unique writing style. Songwriters do not follow a "one size fits all" format.

I point these things out to show how fascinating the process is, and for me the more I write, the less I know. It is a craft full of magical twists and turns. Just because a song is well written does not mean guaranteed wide reception. There have been so many songs that don't follow the rules, yet find their way into the heart of the listener. Go figure.

There are songwriters who write by themselves and find it the most comfortable way for them to create. I can relate to this in one area. In standard songwriting, I enjoy the give and take of ideas with another creative. However, if I'm writing a more through-composed legit composition, my preference is to do that alone. Let's just say that I'm in my "happy place" when I'm writing.

Here is one example of how a song gets written. Phill McHugh and I were talking about big words one day as we sat in a small writing room at the Paragon Publishing building. Phill and I had been friends since the days of producing a couple of his records at Tri-Art Recording in Bismarck, North Dakota. He was born into an Irish Catholic farming family near Aberdeen, South Dakota. Through our own separate journeys, we both ended up in Nashville, he as a writer and me as a producer/songwriter.

In the daily grind of a writing session one day, our discussion focused in on the word, "people." That seemed a big and expansive thought and evoked so many possibilities. We loved how Bob Merrill's lyric, "People," set by Jules Styne was so beautifully delivered by Barbra Streisand. "People who need people" was the phrase that grabbed our attention. We talked for a while, and then it was time for lunch.

We walked over to one of our favorite noontime haunts, where other hopefuls, who were also trying to hunt down those pesky words that scrambled like mice when the room light was turned on, also dined. Our waitress came to the table with perfunctory greeting, we joked with her and she laughed, took our order, and walked off.

There was something very peculiar about her presence. It seemed her eyes betrayed the dutiful smile. Something just wasn't right, something subtly askew. We looked at each other and said, "She needs the Lord today." We kept on with the thought and continued. "Hey, we need the Lord just as much." Who knew what she was going through. She could be a single mother whose husband had left her with three children, and she was working two jobs to stay afloat. You just don't know what other people have to deal with. We went on with our meal and both of us were quietly taking in the whole of the scenario. What did this episode in our life mean? That's what songwriters do. Observe and then tell the story as they see it, looking out their creative window.

As we left the restaurant, we looked at each other, and almost simultaneously said to each other, "Are you thinking what I'm thinking?" That big word, "people," came soaring back into our minds and "People Need the Lord" was being subconsciously written as we walked back to our writing room. Within twenty minutes came the opening verse and chorus.

Everyday they pass me by,
I can see it in their eyes.
Empty people filled with care,
Headed who knows where?
On they go through private pain,
Living fear to fear.

Laughter hides their silent cries,
Only Jesus hears.

People need the Lord, people need the Lord.
At the end of broken dreams, He's the open door.
People need the Lord, people need the Lord.
When will we realize people need the Lord?

You never know where a song you've written will end up. When US Air Flight 427 crashed near Pittsburg, Pennsylvania in 1994, all 132 passengers were killed. Eleven days earlier a young man who was on the flight had just sung a song written by Phill McHugh and me entitled, "As We Sail to Heaven's Shore." The news media brought attention to this and the song was played at the memorial service. The lyrics are now enshrined on a huge stone monument at the crash site.

Well, surely, what we love rests comfortably in the living room of our soul. We don't exactly know how our passions find their way to our heart because most often they arrive in great mystery. We take pictures of life and articulate them in poetry, art, music, and performance as we look out our individual creative window.

Some of us are loathe in sharing our creations for fear of rejection, yet we have this inner longing to express what we see and feel in life. With the best description we can muster, we write, rewrite, struggle, experiment, fail, and live in unconscious, pulsating angst in an enigmatic blend of profuse frustration and bliss.

There are some who have been given great gifts in one area and have an abundance of natural talent, but don't use it. Some with much less ability are tireless in honing the abilities they have, in pursuit of working at 100 percent capacity, and to great effect.

In the changing landscape that is the music industry, I've had many producers, artists, and songwriters—some young, some seasoned—sit with me in my writing room, pouring out their consternation about the unfairness of the business. I understand the frustration of not being heard, but I also know what's at its root. Ultimately, these feelings are seeds of economic bitterness festering in a pool of wanton significance. It's particularly born out in individuals who had tremendous early success but can no longer make a living as a songwriter. Embittered, they rail on the "business" with some notion of everlasting entitlement. There are seasons in our life and we have to come to terms with changing times because if we don't, the alternative is to spend our life with an underlying seething resentment.

I believe that each of us is given a measure of talent by God, and how that is exacted, I couldn't tell you. The problem is that some are not content with the measure of gift they have been given, or ignore the fact that songwriting may not be their strongest gift. Another thing I avoid is making comparisons about something so subjective as well-crafted songs. It reminds me of the running joke my sister told me about choral conductors. It goes like this. The only thing on which two choral conductors can agree is the inadequacy of the third.

Probably the most difficult crossroad for anyone looking at a songwriting career, is dealing with the possibility that they simply do not have a gifting in this area. There is nothing wrong with writing for pleasure. For some it is absolutely cathartic. The real test is being able to come to the conclusion that Clint Eastwood came to in the movie *Magnum Force*. "A man's got to know his limitations."

26

"THEN SHALL THE EYES OF THE BLIND BE OPENED"

One of the most interesting chapters of my life occurred in the year 1988. I went on a three-week trip to visit Ecuador, Argentina, Columbia, and Venezuela with artist friend, Steve Green, his family, and a songwriting buddy, Jon Mohr. Steve's parents were missionaries in Venezuela and he had grown up in Argentina until in his late teens moving stateside. This would be an unforgettable trip on many levels.

We landed in Quito, Ecuador, and traveled on to the small town of Shell, Ecuador. This little town was near the home of Rachel Saint, the sister of Nate Saint, one of five missionaries who were speared to death by members of an Auca Indian settlement near a place called Palm Beach in January of 1956. This action was reported and featured in a ten-page colored photo *LIFE* magazine article, as well as many other print publications including *Reader's Digest*. Hearing the background of these missionaries was deeply meaningful to me, not only because of the tragic element of the account, but in learning about the healing reunion between the actual people who had executed the five men and the families of those martyred missionaries. As a result, I became mindful of existing tensions related to western cultural imposition in the name of faith upon ancient indigenous people groups.

As I stood on a small airstrip close by Rachel's home, I heard a voice excitedly calling my name and turned to see who it was. It was the son of one of the missionaries in the area and he held out a cassette tape. I'm in the middle of nowhere in Ecuador and this kid is pitching me a song to cut on one of my artists. It didn't matter where I went, commerce was still plenty alive. On that same airstrip, I saw a bunch of men huddled around a small cardboard box. As I came closer I saw they were watching a huge tarantula spider. Just as I got up to see what it was, this furry spider jumped up in the box and I immediately saw my life pass before me. Man o man o man o man!!!!!

While we were in Ecuador, we stayed at a hotel on the city square of Shell. There was a nice restaurant right next to it and the food was delicious—that is if you could ignore the four monkeys that were running around the place and splashing in the little fountain on one side of the room. One of these little creatures definitely had been drinking way too much prune juice and was excitedly "spreading the joy" wherever he went. I just tried not to imagine the health reality while eating my entrée. I had high hopes that I would not have to experience any lower tract issues so apparently displayed by the little monkey I affectionately named "Squirt."

My second-story hotel room was extremely spacious, but stark. The walls held no art, there was a large dresser that sat next to a very tiny bathroom and a small bed in the middle of the room seemed dwarfed by the bigness of the room. This room also had a balcony to the outside and you could see vendors across the street selling fruit, vegetables, jewelry, hats, and other trinkets.

This is where one of the most meaningful moments in my life occurred. I heard people singing in the marketplace and walked out on the balcony.

They were having a little church service right in the middle of the day, and to my utter astonishment they were singing one of my songs in Spanish. I stood there; numb. To think that what I felt in my heart was also something to which another people group in the world could relate. Yes, I cried as I listened, and those tears were grateful streams. God was allowing me to enjoy the gift He had given my writing partner, Phill McHugh, and me.

The next excursion we took was to the mountains of Ecuador. We flew in an MAF (Mission Aviation Fellowship) plane to view an area called "Palm Beach" where the five missionaries had been martyred. We continued our flight to the top of a great mountain, landing on a dirt airstrip in the middle of a deeply forested area. We were informed that without a plane, it would have taken a three-day hike to get to this village. As we got out of the plane, a very skinny and shirtless little man ran up to us brandishing a wide toothless smile. In a very short time, we realized he was looking for us to purchase the necklaces dangling on his arm. While he motioned and chattered, we noticed a strong scent of alcohol. Not wanting to be impolite, I paid the price he was asking, knowing my wife would totally understand that this was no time for value shopping.

Scanning the open yard, I noticed women sitting around a big pot with a fire blazing underneath. It was filled with a milky substance called chichi. These women would take a bite of a cleaned up root from a Yucca plant, chew it for a while, and spit into a big pot that was sitting on a bed of burning logs. Then with their hands take out the remaining fibrous part still lodged in their mouth, and later scoop out the milky liquid from the boiling pot and put it in another container.

Soon the little skinny guy came up with a bowl of this chichi and offered us all a drink. So here's the deal, this chichi has got to be 200 proof alcohol, and it's a staple for these people. As a result, it's no wonder they were smiling all the time, they were all lit up like Macy's Christmas tree.

While we were in the mountains we went on a hike and crossed a little creek. My feet got soaked, but I didn't think anything of it.

From Ecuador we traveled to Salta, Argentina. When we got in country, we discovered that there was one small problem; the country was experiencing a coup. We were not allowed to leave the place where we were staying. We found out that this was not unusual; they had these little coups from time to time. Well . . . how refreshing.

When things subsided we continued to the place where Steve and David were raised. Venturing up into the mountains of Argentina, we came upon an area where some of the indigenous Indians were selling their wares. I came to one gentleman who was selling a musical instrument called a charango. This member of the lute family is a ten stringed instrument (with five sets of coupled strings). At the time, the body of the instrument was built with an armadillo shell, however using these animals for this use has now been outlawed. I purchased a charango from an Argentinian luthier, and to this day my granddaughters each take their turn with it whenever they make music in our piano room.

At nightfall, our group drove to the very top of this mountain in Argentina and came to a huge hotel that appeared closed. Steve told us that it had served as a retreat center for missionaries in the area. They would come there for rest, downtime, and encouragement from each other. This was another spectacular moment for all of us. When we tried knocking on the door, it opened and the owners greeted us.

They were staying there until it was time to re-open for the new tourist season. They told us they would be glad to prepare dinner for us, and a fantastic meal it was. We talked with them for at least two or three hours. At one point, the lady who was hosting said, "I would love to show you something I know you will like. We followed her out of the hotel and walked up a short incline and came to a grassy area at the top of the mountain. It was as close to a star as I had ever been. There was absolutely no light pollution and it seemed as if you could touch these huge stars. My eyes marveled as I lay on the soft grass for the next hour. I couldn't get enough of this truly heavenly sight.

We only spent two days in Bogota, Columbia, because it was a little iffy in terms of safety. Onward to Caracas, Venezuela, where we met with Steve and David Green's missionary parents.

Throughout our time in South America there was definitive evidence of the very rich and very poor, with little if any middle class. Now this was 1988 and that was my grasp at the time. Once, while I was in Ecuador, an indigenous Indian couple walked up to me, speaking emphatically while pushing their little boy toward me. This young child could not have been more than three years old. When I asked David what they were saying, he told me they were asking me to take their son to America because good things were there. I couldn't speak Spanish and really didn't know what to say, so David took over for me and kindly told them that this was not possible. I'll leave you to put your head around that. To me, it was sobering and unsettling.

After our time of concerts in Venezuela, we were ready to go home. Preparing to leave, I noticed as I took off my socks there was a brown ring forming around my ankle. I didn't know what it would mean until much later.

It was wonderful to get back home to family and normalcy, but it wouldn't last long. Within the next two days I was off to complete a Christmas recording in Los Angeles for one of my most favorite artists of all time, Evelyn Tornquist Karlsson. Evie. I love her special Norwegian hugs! It was a glorious time for me, both musically and spiritually. Evie and her husband, Pelle, have taught me so much about real faith and commitment.

I flew back to Nashville, and on my drive home from the airport I thought I got something in my eye and it wouldn't go away. It bothered me that evening and it seemed to get worse. When I woke up in the morning, I couldn't see anything. I could see light in the corner of my eye, but that was it. I usually never run out of things to say, but I was alarmed and speechless. We made a frantic call to an eye specialist, and soon found out he was not very special.

When we arrived for my appointment, he gave me a steroid shot in my eye . . . yep. Oh my, I was in pain, depressed, and scared all rolled up in one pathetic bundle. He cavalierly told Pam and me, "It doesn't look too good, and I don't know what to do for you." He proceeded to walk out of the examining room, dismissing us with no treatment, no referral, no nothing. We were like deflated emotional balloons. I couldn't see my wife, my kids, my friends, and that was that.

Pam became proactive and found the best eye specialist at Vanderbilt Clinic. Months of pictures and research on rare eye diseases and conditions ensued. The best guesses were either a South American parasite or possibly Epstein-Barr, but no diagnosis was ever pinpointed. There was scarring over the macula, holes in the retina, and that's about all I knew. I had to stay busy and keep my spirits up. Pam and the kids were depending on me, so this was no time to bathe in self-pity.

We sold my car and my production assistant, Cindy Wilt, drove me everywhere. Musician friends picked me up often and it was the session players who really came to my aid. We bought a nice condominium on Music Row so if sessions ran late and I couldn't get a ride, I had a place to stay. Cindy read all my correspondence as well as the Bible to me. My neighbor, Jeff McWaters, was in health care and traveling all the time, but every morning he would call from wherever he was in the country, read the Bible, and pray with me. To me, his love was a continual quiet hug, not calling attention to itself. The record companies were unbelievably kind. I lost no artists and work continued. I know that I am an effusive person, that's how I roll, but how could I not be effusive in thankfulness to my community of friends in Nashville, Los Angeles, and London. They all came alongside me. That's what I had hoped, and that's how it was. My church also encouraged me. They had a special service of prayer for all those who desired it. There was no way I was going to miss this opportunity. It was a wonderful time of prayer and really a time of inner healing that brought me out of a fearful state into one of gratitude, thinking of others, and the joy of all I was learning about myself and what God was teaching me.

The most unbelievable response I received came from a treasured mentor back home in Bismarck. This man, Harold Schafer, was a successful businessman, entrepreneur, and benefactor. Throughout the years he had given so much to enrich our state, helping needy students financially who wanted to go to college, families in distress and many more instances than I have room to write. He was no respecter of status and I was one of the many grateful recipients of his continual kindness.

Upon hearing of my blindness, I received a letter from him with this one portion that will stay with me for the rest of my life. He wrote, *"Greg, I'm old now but my eyes still work quite well. However, I don't need them and I can get by. I would be happy for you to have them if there is any way this could be accomplished."* As Pam read his letter to me I couldn't quit sobbing. That was the measure of this man and his love for me. When I visited with his wife, Sheila, she confirmed that he was dead serious and calling around to see if there was any possibility of getting it done. I'll just leave you to ponder the phrase *"no greater love"* and this beautiful picture of the word *"sacrifice."*

I continued a relentless schedule of recordings for months, but after the prayer service at my church, something happened as I was working with Sandi Patty. She was recording vocals at Pine Brook Studios in Alexandria, Indiana, and as I sat at the console; I began to see movement and a faint image of her standing at the microphone. I rose up and started blinking my eyes, thinking to myself this was probably like a mirage people see in the desert when they get loopy from the heat. No, I didn't suddenly see, but within two weeks, my sight began returning and I was able to get around without any help.

We called our wonderful eye doctor at Vanderbilt and made a quick appointment. He took more photos of my eyes and came back to us with these very words, "What church do you go to?" He continued to say, "Well there probably is a medical explanation for this, but at this point I'm really not sure what that is. " He had been studying this intensely, following anything remotely like my condition in medical journals and calling colleagues all over the world.

Sight did not return in my right eye, but my left eye cleared enough so I could read and drive . . . although my wife thinks I drive like a blind man anyway. This was such an overwhelming season in my life that I've never written a song relating to it or told many people about it. Some people like to use occurrences like this as fodder for the theatrical. For me, my recovery has been a deeply personal chapter and I would not want to see it cheapened in any way.

I am amazed at God's great love and kindness toward me. He has watched over me, comforted me, and healed me, among so many other blessings. This is why I believe so much in the power of prayer. This event clarified my faith and let me see how powerful God is and how powerless I really am to control that runaway horse. I don't know a whole lot, but I know this. Once I was blind and now I can see.

You don't get through something like this without your family surrounding you and giving you strength to push through. I couldn't have had a better family to do just that.

27

MY FAMILY

"Hey, mister. Get off my driveway!" So flew the words from the mouth of my three-year old, Ben, as the mailman approached our house to deliver the mail one snowy day. Ben was full of vim and vinegar and we never knew what was coming next. Sarah, our first-born was the typical first born, compliant and wouldn't think of causing us a moment of trouble for any reason.

My wife, Pam, was a constant presence in our children's lives. I was literally gone for days at a time except to sleep. I hasten to add that I never missed an event for either child. If I was in the studio, I rearranged my hours to attend baseball, basketball, or musical activities in which Sarah and Ben participated. There is always a price to pay if you want to do something well. I didn't mind the work, but I did not want to be a distant father or husband. Pam was understanding and did not bemoan the schedule, but would become angered if I had time off and was inattentive. As the children grew up, she put up with so much in those years of school, doctor's appointments, church, homework, music lessons, and special activities.

She was not a lover of the music business and I could definitely understand her feelings. Pam saw the raw side of the business with questionable business practices, some needy artists, and executives who sought attention at any cost. She was able to see through the façade of many individuals in all aspects of the business with whom I worked. In addition, it was the industry that took me away from her on so many occasions.

Pam's own childhood was one with working parents. She wanted to make sure that her children would not suffer the same loss as she had with parents often too busy for her. This was burned into her memory and she was motivated to be a deeply caring mother with great attention to detail. She was that and more.

It is one thing to deal with a busy schedule as Pam did, but she had an even more difficult task in dealing with an eccentric and obsessive-compulsive husband with teeming peculiarities. As odd as it may seem, I thought I was pretty normal, thinking everyone was like me. Oh, brother, was I completely mistaken. I had never been diagnosed, and when I finely understood this condition, things finally made sense. I could not take medication because my greater family had a potent history of addiction.

Pam has been so patient with me, but of course cannot relate remotely to ADHD. She always asks me what I am thinking because she knows me. We'll be driving along and she'll calmly ask me, "Where are you now?" or "Who are you talking to?" It's kinda bizarre, but that's our life. Another question she asked me was how I feel in my skin. I told her that it is like being in a continual state of an adrenalin rush even when I am resting.

We attended Brentwood Baptist Church for some twenty plus years, and because they were growing so much, a move to a larger facility was sorely needed. This new sanctuary was huge and all the issues of my disorder came into account. During congregational prayer I'd try to be attentive , but I always ended up saying to myself, "Shut up, just shut up."

I was over stimulated and distracted by what I saw in the sanctuary. It could be anything. Eventually I realized that this wasn't working for me any longer and I had to do something about it. These were families whom Pam and I loved. Our children had grown up with these people and our daughter's family still attends there.

We were invited by a friend to visit a much smaller church closer to Nashville and further away from Brentwood. This was a huge deal for Pam and me. Now I'm asking her to consider a different church for my sake. We attended Judson Baptist Church and quickly fell in love with the pastor, his wife, and the congregation. Pam once again made a sacrifice for me. I'm crying right now as I write. Such gracious love she has for our entire family and me! Don't get me wrong, we go head to head many times, but at the end of it all . . . love . . . always love.

It was a steamy hot August day. Ben and I were sitting out front of our home as we waited for Pam to get in the car. We both were getting a little impatient. All of a sudden I hear these words screaming from Ben. *"Where is that dumb mom!"* I turned around and stared at him as he sat in his car seat. Before I could say a word, with wide eyes he blurted out, "Who said that?" I replied, "Yah, who said that?" Just as quickly as I asked, he had his faithful response. "Copper." Copper was our dog. Whenever Ben was caught in anything, he blamed the dog. That dog was a prolific offender, even capable of stealing change from the kitchen counter. He must have had an unbelievable vertical jump.

When Ben was about five years old, Pam took him to the doctor's office. He tried to jump up on the examining table and bumped his knee. This was followed by his utterance of a classic swear word. Pam was in tears and Ben was once again in a familiar place—trouble.

When they got home he was put in time out and sat on a little kid's chair in the middle of our rec room. When I got home, Pam, teary eyed and disgusted, told me to immediately get in the room and take care of the situation. I tried to be cool, walked in and said. "Ben, you might think I'm mad, but I'm not. I have to tell you though just how very disappointed I am in you. Immediately he turned to me and said, "Yah, dad, just for one little . . . and he repeated the word again. He didn't get it and it was hard for me to keep a straight face. "Who taught you that word, Ben." Yep. You're right. It was our dog, Copper.

Ben was a little pistol, but when he was in middle school at about age fourteen, we were looking at a video project he was in and we couldn't believe our eyes. He looked like an Auschwitz victim. We were horrified. We were used to seeing him daily and didn't see his weight loss immediately.

One day there was a call from the school nurse who informed us that she was having a hard time keeping him awake. We immediately took him to the emergency room and after taking his blood, the doctor told us to get him to the hospital immediately. His blood sugar was skyrocketing and he was in trouble. He was diagnosed with type 1 diabetes. As he was being instructed how to give himself an insulin shot for the first time, I was at a breaking point. I walked out of the room in a tearful mess and as I turned into the hall I bumped into something and looked up. It was an IV post on wheels.

Standing next to it was the cutest little bald headed girl no older than seven or eight. She was smiling at me and immediately I knew it was God speaking to me again through one of his little messengers. "Greg, you don't have any problems. Take note of this precious lovely, Ben will be just fine." I got the message, wiped my tears away, and went back to Ben's room. Ben has done a great job of remaining healthy and his life goes on.

I have many close friends, but my son, Ben, is the man I feel closest to in my life. I remember the day he was born and his dedication in the church. I appreciate his winning personality, his love of music, his accomplishments, and the great joy he brings both Pam and me as we watch him care for his family so well. I love when he teases me and I enjoy irritating him. It is a beautiful heartfelt bond.

When we moved to California, Sarah was two years old. It was easy to bring her to events because she was content to listen and play with whatever toy we brought along for her. When she was a little over three years old, we took her to a park to swing, slide, and picnic. She absolutely loved this time and was repeatedly going down the little slide near where we were sitting. But in a flash, she scampered over to a giant slide further away from us with a long stretch of steps to the top. She began climbing up the ladder and as we were walking toward her, she fell back and landed on her head. *We were frantic.* Many parents have had similar experiences at some time in their children's adventurous lives.

We rushed her to the emergency room and were met with very good care, but in the process it was apparent to us that they were suspicious we might have harmed her. This is understandable in view of all the horrendous stories of child abuse. We answered their questions and she was finally ready to go home. We were greatly relieved that she was going to be okay and relaxed a little more as we drove home. At home, we were to give her baby aspirin a certain amount of times a day, so we kept them close on the kitchen counter. Well here's where it gets interesting . . . I mean frightening.

Sarah decided she liked the flavored aspirin she was taking, took the pills into her room, and started to finish off the bottle. When we realized what had happened, we were freaking out once again and rushed her to the same hospital where the same doctor and nurses were still on duty.

This did not look good for the home team. We walked in and told them what had happened and they gave her medication to make her throw up. Now they were looking at us like we were relatives of nurse Ratchet. This time the questions were quite intense, more forceful, and looked like it was going to be "slammer time" for Greg and Pam. After much explanation they decided that we might be telling them the truth and we were allowed to take her home without incident.

Sarah (who I call "Tweety") is the consummate loving daughter and the woman I most admire, next to her mother. A picture of beauty and a natural born nurturer, she is over the top in her concern for the rightful treatment of everyone she meets. Sarah's love of new horizons, music, and friends are an example to me. She is dutiful mother and a loving wife. Both Ben and Sarah have married two amazing partners. Pam and I cannot adequately express our thankfulness to God for bringing Emily and Damian into their lives. They are truly a living treasure to our family.

Pam and I are exact opposites. She's organized and methodical and I'm—well I'm a mess. We get along. She tells me what I need to do (which she needs to do) but I don't like her telling me what I need to do. She tells me what to do anyway. Now that I've cleared that up, she really does need to remind me about stuff because my short-term memory is getting very bad . . . and so is my short-term memory.

We were sitting in a movie theater the other day and she said, "Honey, what's the name of that place in England we were talking about last week? You know the one with . . . you know . . . it's got ruins and it's a rock thingy out in the middle of nowhere or something like that." So I'm thinking, *we just talked about it last week?* I've got *no* clue. (Just for the record, I can't remember what I had for breakfast much less what I talked about last week.) I can tell she feels I should be able to retrieve this one easily. (This is a very bad omen for me.)

Let's see. Now that she had clearly shined the light on what it was, you know, a rock thingy out in the middle of nowhere, and of course in "wife-speak" that meant, "I've given you enough information, do I have to draw you a map?" Suddenly, the hamsters that work second shift in my mind (they're union) started running like crazy and the wheel began spinning. I was fortunate they were maniacally dutiful, because all of a sudden I knew what she was talking about. That scene from "Spinal Tap" where this backdrop comes down representing this place, but it's only a miniature scale version of it. A very funny scene from that movie. But I digress (as usual).

I've been to England many times. I know the name of this place, but sixty-plus years of synapse wear and tear was setting in. I knew for sure that it started with the letter "H" but maybe not, that was about as far as I could get. I started going down the alphabet and making up words that sounded English to me, and with discovery might possibly render me potent. Nothing. The movie started and I was in turmoil.

As the movie was playing, Pam looked at me and said, "You're not watching the movie, are you?" I told her, "Yes, I am." She said, "Where are you, Greg? Where did you go?" I told her I was somewhere off the coast of England. Then she got after me and told me to knock it off and watch the movie. I had to know. I excused myself and said I had to use the bathroom. I walked out of the theater and over to the men's restroom and began to Google it. Within a matter of a minute or two I had the answer. I was so excited, I turned and smiled at the guy standing at the urinal next to me and muttered, "*Yes!*" I don't know why I did that, but it was incredibly awkward. He looked at me like, "Mister, you're scaring me," and left hurriedly. I walked back into the theater and ran up the stairs to where my wife was sitting.

I turned to her with giddy excitement, and at the same time she smiled and said, "Stonehenge." I'm in counseling now, and I really think I'm getting a lot better.

Within our family there is great respect for each other no matter political, religious, or any other view. We get together as often as we can and we always make beautiful memories. My brother, sister, and I are particularly close, and I often describe my relationship with my sister as my twin born in a different year. My brother is quieter than his frenetic siblings and he lovingly puts up with our peculiarities. The cousins and cousins once removed are beautifully bonded.

My family is a safe place for me, with no fear of judgment. Thru the tragic loss of my niece, Holly Nelson, numerous serious illnesses, and personal difficulties, our family has always surrounded the suffering ones and no one is ever left comfortless. With an underlying "musical hum" ever-present, each of us are tethered to this tight knit clan. Our pets have also been a source of great joy as well. Many times it was our sweet dogs that got us all through some difficult hours and days.

28

A PARTING TALE

You know they say you could throw your wife and your dog in the trunk of your car, drive around the city for an hour, and when you stop and let them out, your wife would want to kill you . . . but your dog . . . well your dog would just be happy to see you again. Your dog worships you . . . your cat tolerates you. I like this anonymous quote. "Look in my eyes and deny it. No human could love you as much as I do." That was my Katie until the day she died.

She was a soft-eyed cock-a-poo, with a black coat, long body, supremely guileless and of compliant gentle temperament. Her eyes were just like those you see in commercials, you know those images of the sad-eyed puppies with the mournful Sarah McLachlan song playing in the background. That was the look of our little Katie. How we loved her: Sarah, Ben, Pam, and me. She was always there for us—a cuddling balm in difficult times. Content to lie in your lap and be snuggled, her eyes exuded a continual sweetness and a contented disposition that few humans are able to find.

It's no coincidence that man's best friend can't talk. When nobody was around, I'd talk to her, always wondering how much of what I was saying she understood . . . but she never did talk back to me. If work was difficult, if you were at odds with your family, if you were sick, if the world was closing in on you, or you were losing hope, you could always count on three things: the Lord, Katie, and a quart of Rocky Road ice cream.

When our grandchildren started to appear at the house, Katie was a loving friend. The kids were frightened at first, but Katie was patient with them, and when any unintentional awkward fur pulling or roughness presented itself, Katie would simply walk away. We did have to keep the children from mimicking Katie as she stuck her hind legs out in front of her, dragging her butt on the carpet across the length of the room.

She could express more with her stubby tail in a minute, than most people can express in hours. I wouldn't say she made a great guard dog. I'm pretty sure the only way we would know that we had a prowler in our home, would be if said intruder fell over Katie as she slept. His only penalty? Being thoroughly licked to distraction.

But Katie would never have been in the picture had it not been for the very first dog my children had. We found Copper shortly after we moved to Nashville. Like Katie, she was a cock-a-poo, black and thoroughly lovable. Sarah named her "Copper," the dog's name in the movie *The Fox and the Hound*.

At sixteen years of age, Copper began to fail, which began discussions between Pam and me about if and when we would have to put her to sleep. Finally, the day came when we brought the kids together and broke the news. Copper had no real quality of life and it was obvious even to our children. We informed them that I would be taking her to the vet the following day and they would not see her again. I don't need to inform anyone who has ever owned a pet what scene ensued.

Throughout our home there was a heart-wrenching pall with intermittent bursts of tears from Ben and Sarah as they mourned for this little life that had calmed their fears, played with them ever since they could play, and somehow helped them forget for a moment just how bad they felt when they were sick.

Copper, their constant companion in life, wouldn't be there for them anymore. The next morning was a gray overcast morning. Ben, Sarah, Pam, and I walked around in a dazed perfunctory swim as we prepared for the day. It was time and the kids said their goodbyes through red, swollen eyes, continually looking back as they walked away, their gaze fixed on Copper.

I loaded Copper in the car for her final ride to the vet's office and carried her in amidst all the vibrancy of other wagging tails in the office. I looked at her, comforting her as she feebly licked my hand. I was hoping she was saying to me, "Hey, it's alright. It's time; I know." They say that a dog knows when they are going to die. In my heart of hearts, I really think she did. I can hardly get this story out. I'm sitting here . . . staring . . . with a lump in my throat. Old friends—pets are, with a powerful effect on our lives. They teach us things about ourselves and we become better people. I aspire to their disposition and faithfulness.

"Copper Nelson," the lady at the door said. We walked into the vet's examining room and there were towels on the hard cold steel examining table for Copper to lie down on. The vet walked in, we talked about her condition and he concurred with our family decision. "Would you like a few minutes with her, he asked?" We said our goodbyes with words, my tears, and looks. I kissed her and petted her for the last time, turned, and closed another chapter in my life as I shut the door behind me.

Two days later, I was eating breakfast, minding my own business, when Pam asked me where Copper's body was. I told her that the vet was going to have her buried in a mass grave in a real nice dog cemetery. She burst into tears and said, "How could you do that to us?" What? How could I do what to us? I was totally confused.

I guess she was still in a grief state and her feelings were more than pretty close to the surface. She said, "You get back there and bring Copper home, I want her buried in the backyard." There are times in every husband's life when he *must* take a stand! Well, this was not one of them.

How was this going to happen? Oh yeah, I'm just gonna go back to the doctor's office and ask, "Uh, you remember when I came here with Copper and she was put to sleep. I know that I said I wanted her buried in that mass dog grave. Well, I take it back. We want to bury her in the backyard. You haven't buried her yet, have you? Because if you have, I have a shovel in my trunk and I've got some work to do or living in my house will not be tolerable any-more... and that's even *if* I will be able to get back into my house."

I arrived at the vet's office and told them about my dilemma. "Let me check on that for you," replied the woman at the desk, and she walked to a back room. A few minutes later she returned with good news and bad news. Copper had not yet been taken for burial, but there was a slight problem. She was kept in a freezer. She was now frozen with her legs outstretched; they did not have a large enough box to put her in. I asked if she had something close to the right size, and she returned with what appeared to be a box used for flowers. I tried to get Copper all the way in, but her back legs stuck way out. I thanked her and said that the box would be just fine. Just then I got the giggles and couldn't stop laughing.

The picture of me walking out the office with a frozen dog whose legs were sticking out of the end was just too much for me. I tried to control myself, but for me it was an emotional release and all just too bizarre. The crazy Greg in me thought, I'm working this to the hilt, so I walked right out into the waiting room. There was an instantaneous hush. One lady stared at me, pressing her little Shih Tzu even closer to her body. I did not change expression, and in a deadpan look said, "She didn't have a very good appoint-ment," and just kept walking out of the building. I know it wasn't very nice... but could you blame me with an opportunity like that?

29

CARNEGIE HALL

The smell of bread, fresh out of the oven, came rushing to our senses as my family sat at our table at Carmine's in New York. They had come to support and encourage me for the twentieth anniversary performance of *Saviour*, an oratorio I co-wrote with my good friend, Bob Farrell. The performance was at Carnegie Hall and it was beyond anything I could have imagined. It was a full house, ending with a standing ovation and from the stage the promoter acknowledging our vision as composers. He asked us to stand and be recognized. I was humbled. As I stood in my box, the audience did not know the treasure I was holding in my heart.

In attendance were my wife, Pam, my incredible children Sarah and Ben and Ben's wife, Emily, my brother, sister, and their spouses—some of whom had told me they were not coming. There were also some special friends from Texas and my church in Nashville. We were blessed to be hosted by my precious niece, Serena, and her equally gem of a husband, Adam. Their meticulous planning took us from the New York High Line to a ferry ride, a picnic lunch in Central Park, the World Trade Center Memorial and Museum, and concluded with an unforgettable celebration of Ben and Emily's marriage, with a meal of kale and kielbasa (from the Polish neighborhood where they live in Brooklyn—Green Point). Oh, oh! Did I mention Adam's unmatched mac and cheese and the fact that he cooked everything for us?

The last night, we talked, toasted, and told jokes with familial unabashed delivery. Around the table and one on one, loving streams of talk carried spiritual questions, life experiences, and dreams as the deep reverence we felt for each other flowed in and out of our hearts.

As to the work that was performed, I talked to my partner extraordinaire, Bob Farrell, when he got back from the trip. As we shared the joy of having this rare opportunity that Roy Hayes (the chief organizer and promoter) allowed all of us to experience, we fell on one verse that neither one of us had really quite grasped up until this time, Ephesians 3:20. "Now to Him who is able to do far more abundantly beyond all that we ask or think, according to the power that works within us, to Him be the glory in the church and in Christ Jesus to all generations forever and ever. Amen." Standing in front of the crowd was like over the top . . . really almost too much for us. We both expressed the fact that we stood there acknowledging ownership of something it was impossible to take credit for, something that was handed over to us, and pretty much dictated to us. We really didn't know what we were doing. The oratorio was not in the industry mode where we operated. It was difficult for both choir and soloists.

We must have been out of our minds spending two years on something we both thought might never be recorded, much less heard. It didn't make sense to anyone, but we were compelled to write. We did feel we wanted to leave this as a legacy to our children and grandchildren. Through a maze of writing and re-writing, recording sections of the work, eliminating sections that had been recorded; the work came into view. We took the work to every Christian label and were turned down. The labels were use to a certain formula that was successful for them and this work did not fit that mold.

That was understandable. It wasn't until we took the oratorio to Warner-Atlantic headed by Neal Joseph that we found a home. He was a great champion of the work and *Saviour* would never have gotten off the ground without his effort and vision. Word Publishing handled the printed music, and Ken Barker, one of the most brilliant editors in our industry, agreed to edit both the printed book and orchestral score. His work was absolutely meticulous.

In working with orchestrator Ronn Huff and arranger David Hamilton, we all felt as if we all were sitting around the creative fire and warming our hands together. It was an exhilarating time recording in London, standing on the floor, and listening to a run-through among some eighty musicians in CTS Studios (now Phoenix Studios). This was truly one of the most rewarding experiences of my musical life. The raw emotional beauty coming at you in such close proximity is without equal. I have recorded many huge string dates in London, but this one was heavenly. I'll just stop there . . . can't describe it any other way. What I hope you hear me saying is that from a life's work perspective, this would be a pinnacle moment without any hesitation.

At the end of it all, all of our life work, all of our dreams, all of our triumphs, all of our failures, lost opportunities, disillusionment, and all of our want to be loved, there is this: the loving eyes of our family. Whether blood relative or not, whatever family has become for you now, you know, and they know. No matter the miles or years that separate, there comes a faithful acceptance— real and visceral. I can't even qualify the warmth of Ben, Sarah, and Serena coming up to me rubbing my back and saying, "I love you, Dad," "I love you, Poppie," I love you Uncle Greg," "That was awesome, Dad," and getting a kiss right along with the whisper. How does it get any richer than this?

That's what began for me at Carmine's and ended up at Adam and Serena's home in Brooklyn. I was so grateful for the message of the work, the kind encouragement of the audience, and the spectacular presentation by everyone involved in the evening. As we came together to express our love for one another, the joy of this family reunion strengthened the bond between us in an even more meaningful way. This is not the last reunion Pam and I would attend that year. Soon there would be another reunion we were excited about and we could hardly wait for that weekend to arrive.

30

THE CLASS OF 1966 REUNION

Why hello! There was a long pause, and a long look from an old familiar face greeting me as I entered the ballroom for my high school reunion. A quick glimpse of my nametag was followed with a knowing smile. "Greg, it's great to see you again." So many years had passed—fifty, to be accurate. I was exuberant and expectant as I threw my cap in the air at the conclusion of the graduation ceremony for the Bismarck High School Class of 1966. Now I was coming back for a short visit and remembrance of a simpler time.

Memories came in a wash of faces, sounds, tastes, events, and the feelings I felt. I wanted to hold on, however briefly. I wanted to tell each person I saw and with whom I spoke, just how deeply thankful I was to have them in the fabric of my life. I couldn't help but tear up with each photo I took. I was retrieving their image, but saying goodbye to the visceral experience of being present with them. These were treasured moments. I watched groups of these beautiful classmates laugh as they recounted their times together, sometimes accurately and sometimes slightly altered in faded recollection.

In a sense, this was a return to our innocence. It was a time when fists settled matters, when pranks were just pranks, and we all did life together. Maliciousness had great difficulty surviving in this environment because as I said before, we all tended to look out for each other. If there was a dance, movie, athletic event, or whatever, there was a crowd.

So many wonderful hours were spent at the Teen Canteen Dance held upstairs at Hillside Pool on Friday nights as we danced to forty-five rpm records playing from a jukebox. Romance was rampant in the room, and I could easily have thought that I was "going with" any girl who allowed me to dance cheek to cheek with her to the strains of "Oh, Donna." In a testosterone driven love frenzy and the scent of Aquanet in her hair, I listened to the lyrics to the music. Oh, what great feelings and emotions these song lyrics evoked in me. What deep meaning they held.

'Cause I love my girl . . . Donna, where can you be?
Where can you be? Oh, Donna. Oh, Donna . . .

And then, "Baby, you send me . . . oh, you send me." The words were SO deep . . . so, so deep. (Okay, maybe that's a little overreach.)

Well, a band of friends would leave the dance and head out for Doug Johnson's house that was about twenty blocks away. There we would party with pop, chips, and more dancing. On the walk, I might break up with the girl with whom I had left the dance at 10th Street and be "in a relationship" with another girl by about 4th street. These were heavy relationships and not superficial whatsoever. This was not "puppy love." This was unfettered hormonal bliss.

We shared our reunion with the Catholic high school in Bismarck, St. Mary's. We were the Bismarck "Demons" and they were the St. Mary's "Saints" . . . Though I must confess none of us were very "saintly" in high school.

When you have Germans from Russia and Scandinavians in full bloom, you're going to have Protestants and Catholics. We all got along; and there were a lot of mixed (Protestant/Catholic) marriages that survived the passage of time. How do I know these things? I know, because I married a fine young Catholic girl who wanted to be a nun. (But that's a whole 'nother can o' worms.)

And then there were "the quiet things." As I look back and see the world as it was then and is now. North Dakota days were quite different from living in other areas of our country. As I mentioned before, we weren't as attuned to the civil rights sit-ins and protests that were going on in the south. If we were, there was really not much discussion. Where was I? I'm not blaming anyone, but it makes me feel so sad, so ignorant and guilty. Naiveté for sure, I would have raised my voice in dissent if I had known. Living in the south and hearing from the brave ones who spoke out and were beaten, learning of those who died in the cause of freedom has sobered me tremendously.

As to faith, I do not remember my classmates ever talking about deep spiritual issues. Conversations were about what our youth group was doing at the churches we attended, but no real meaningful dialogue. There was no outward expression or questioning faith. Most of our religious fervor was about pancake suppers, Easter early morning services, and Christmas candlelight services. Of course we could always complain about going to catechism.

Sexuality was another quiet subject. Discussion and questions of homosexuality, abortion, transgender, and other issues like those were virtually silent. Many girls had to deal with teenage pregnancy, but you really didn't hear as much about the boy involved.

I had no idea that I had good friends who struggled with sexual identity. I was so naïve that I did not associate a sexual act with any other thing than male, female relationships. This whole matter did not come into focus for me until I was walking with three army buddies to see the final matinee performance of Melba Moore in the Broadway musical *Purlie*.

It was July 4, 1970, and I was stationed at Fort Hamilton in Brooklyn, New York, for advanced infantry training. We were off for the holiday and a few of us decided to go into Manhattan to see *Purlie*. As we walked to the theater district, we could see this big parade coming down 42nd Street. We found out quickly that it was "Gay Liberation Day" in the city and let's just say my eyes were opened. I didn't consider myself prudish, but I got most of my information from the walls in the bathroom and my male friends boasting their latest conquests. My parents sure didn't spill the proverbial beans. That's for sure.

Another quiet topic was kids dealing with alcoholic parents and sexual abuse. Once again, I'm guilty of my ignorance. I think maybe what I'm trying to get out is that although outwardly I saw an idyllic childhood there were teeming issues about which I was totally oblivious.

I want so desperately to say to my fellow classmates that I wish I'd known then what I know now. I'm so sorry if I missed what you were going through. I wish I could have helped you in some way. Helped the hurt. Helped dry the tears I didn't see.

That's what I felt at this reunion and what I saw through the iPhone camera this time around. Some made it through this life in spite of their difficult upbringing . . . some didn't. This time I stopped and remembered those precious friends who are no longer with us, but are now on to better things. I miss them; I miss the classmates I was with at the reunion already.

God bless the Bismarck High School Class of 1966. You each are inextricably bound to my heart with a grateful tether.

31

RETIREMENT

Nobody grows old merely by living a number of years.
We grow old by deserting our ideals. Years may wrinkle the skin,
but to give up enthusiasm wrinkles the soul.

SAMUEL ULLMAN

I was wading in the pool with my wife one day and out of the blue she said, "You don't like what you're doing anymore do you?" That threw me off balance and I had to think for a moment. I guess I really wasn't enjoying the studio like I used to. A woman's intuition is amazing. Wives just know stuff like this. How? I do not know . . . but they do.

She had detected a rumbling frustration in me and she was spot on. There was a storm brewing in me. I was so busy in my career that I was able to stuff away all my pent up feelings related to the abuse I experienced as a child. But when I decided to retire all my feelings came pouring out in anger. I was emotionally shutting down and went out of my way to do anything to shake that monster. Pam, once again, was my earthly angel and she began to help me sort out what I had held back for so long. It took a lot of prayer and counseling to get a grip on what I was feeling. I hear this pain in the music and lyrics I've written. They really are my life message, these songs of mercy, reassurance, and the need to know God. You don't hear a lot of up-tempo feel good songs coming from my pen. It's just not how I roll.

I'm grateful to God for walking me through the valley of the shadow. Although from time to time my mind and heart rise up in protest. Then, I deal with it once more and life moves on.

Just before I retired, the market that I once knew had moved toward a genre known as "worship music." This was not the musical and lyrical pasture in which I grazed. Churches began implementing worship bands. Choirs disappeared. I want to keep it simple here. There are far better minds than mine that can speak to all the sociological, musical, and theological reasons for this change in direction. I'm just not that smart. Artists found it more difficult to find churches in which to sing and minister. Bottom line: it was a new day.

I had longstanding relationships with the artists I worked with but I began to see that my ideas were getting redundant and tired . . . and I wasn't serving them well no matter how hard I tried. I knew it was time for me to end a very wonderful career and I felt good about it. Gone were the days when I'd find new talent and develop it. Breaking an artist from a recording company perspective was getting increasingly difficult. As this transition was becoming more apparent, I heard complaining about the bleakness of the market. Many artists and writers didn't like the music that was coming out and they made no bones about it. This old guard was still trying to produce material that was no longer connecting as before. What they didn't realize was publishers and recording companies were drastically impacted in both good and bad ways by technology. There was absolutely no doubt that worship music was here to stay and a younger generation was delivering that message. Seasons pass; life moves on.

It was now that I had three clear choices. I could hang on to a dying genre and die with it, I could start chasing a genre for which I had no passion, or I could follow my heart and keep expressing what God was giving me to do. So began one of the most fulfilling periods of my life. Looking back at my beginnings, I remembered individuals who had gone out of their way to support me in my

musical development. People like North Dakota visionary businessman, philanthropist Harold Schafer and his beautiful wife,
Sheila. These were people who had given so much to me and I
realized that it was time for me to pay it forward.

This new season would be one of mentoring young talent in
the US, Russia, India, and Taiwan. Now my days are filled with
writing music and books that I love without worrying about record and publishing companies. Producing is over for me. My
hearing is becoming ever more suspect and my eyesight is failing
at a quick pace. I enjoy being a sounding block for producer and
writer friends in the studio. I don't miss the intensity of what
once was, yet grateful for what the industry has enabled me to do
and create. Gratitude gives me a sweet freedom, hope, and a continued look forward to what the future will bring. I am now able
to enjoy the fruit springing from a lifetime of my labors. These
are the richest of years and getting closer to the day when I'll be
finally home. My life is about today—not yesterday. Pam's and
my greatest ministry and effort is to our grandchildren. Nothing
surpasses that.

In the winter of my life I deal with old people maladies. I'm
living with cancer for now, and my life is one big doctor's appointment. Everyone that has or has had cancer views it differently. I see
it as a nuisance with continual wondering of what's coming next.
There certainly is no fear of death because I know where I am going
without any doubt. And guess what? We all get our turn. As my
pastor, Gene Mims, said, "Death runs in my family." True.

This book is really just a look back at my life, seeing how God
has orchestrated each step I've taken. I see the theater of my life;
the stress and strain as well as the triumphs and warm remembrances. I've learned by watching the lives of my mother and moth-
er-in-law. Both now have passed at the age of 95. I don't know if I
have 95 years in me, but that's a whole other discussion.

Pam and I were right in the middle of the aging action with our
mothers and it was a beautiful time with days of anxiety as well.

I wrote this observance as we lived through the final chapters of these women.

INVISIBLE

Invisible. That's what becomes of them, the elderly. Isn't that awful? That's what we say to ourselves. There it is, end of sentence. It's a faded muse as we look out our window and see unrestrained mobile opportunity and hope with the wind at our back.

The elderly (not all, but many) look out their window and remember what they once dreamed, what they once accomplished and what they once experienced. But now, the hours turn slowly. Life isn't like it used to be. Food doesn't taste like it once did, the aura of their dwelling is strange and familiar faces fall victim to the actuarial tables.

Memory wanes and redundant questions imply a creeping debility. Waiting marks their days. They wait, always waiting, waiting for meals, waiting for family, waiting for calls. Simple tasks become increasingly difficult and frustrating.

Privileges, like driving, are taken from them, and they feel like a changeling. They want to tell the doctor how they feel, but they don't hear well and the conversation is cumbersome and difficult for everyone. They don't want their friends or children to speak for them as in absentia. They have long since given up engaging in group conversation, or much of any conversation for that matter. There is an angst in their psyche that we can't fully grasp. They are slowly disappearing . . . invisible.

My mother passed away before Pam's mother. They had separate issues. My mother's mind was very sharp to the very end, but her body was weak. Mae, Pam's mother was physically very strong, but her mind was overtaken by dementia.

In my mother's final years and months, she continued to hold to her strong faith in what God was doing. She often told me that she was knocking on heaven's door, but He just wouldn't let her in, so she just continued praying for her family and friends. She was a woman of prayer and faithfully intentional in her prayer life. She'd been a widow for thirty-nine years. She moved to Minnesota soon after Dad died to be with my sister Sigrid and her family.

My brother, a luthier, built a violin for her and named it "Irene." We flew from Nashville to Northfield, Minnesota, just a little before she died and took Mom into the chapel of her nursing home to play hymns for her. My sister on piano, my brother on the violin he created, and me on cello. Mother sang to us as we played, her voice was weak, but accompanied with her smile and each of our instruments met with tears.

You can't really adequately describe those moments. It was like out of a movie: a lovely farewell and an impassioned thank you of sorts. Full circle then, and only once in a lifetime to feel that.

It was a learning time for our children, our grandchildren, and us. The greatest joy for both great grandmothers was the sight of their great grandchildren. They both immediately lit up when they came to visit. All of my daughter's three chipmunks (that's what I call my granddaughters) visited their "GG" (Great Grandmother) every other day in the last months of her life. It was a most beautiful and loving gift to behold. They would walk into the facility where Mae lived and greet the other residents with smiles, hugs, and conversation. Tessa Evangeline was four, Magnolia Blythe was seven, and Georgia Corene was eleven.

One day we went to visit Mae and she was completely unresponsive to us for the entire time. Later that day we called Sarah and told her that if she was planning to go, she wouldn't have too much success in eliciting a response. As we spoke, she informed us that she was already there and the children were playing a game with GG. Such was the power of those precious ones.

The most poignant moment in the memorial service was her granddaughters reading their thoughts about GG. They spoke of standing by her bedside right before she died.

Like angels, they tearfully stroked her hair and told her how much they loved her. She was but a shell then, yet to them she was the love of their lives. We'd been waiting the birth of our fourth grandchild, hoping GG would be able to see her.

This was the daughter of our son, Ben, and his lovely wife, Emily. Well, Maya June Nelson was born just days before her passing. Sarah and GG's little chipmunks showed her a picture of her newest great granddaughter. She turned, looked up, and saw Maya's picture and spoke her last word ever on this earth. It was the same word we described that day we celebrated her life, with a soft North Dakota breeze gently whispering through the gravesite. "Beautiful."

I love this piece that my dear friend, Dan Scott wrote about this period in our lives.

> *Nothing is permanent; maturity is about knowing when to let go. We injure ourselves and others trying to hang on to old seasons, to our children as they once were, to our careers as we have experienced them, to positions of authority we have become accustomed to managing and with which we have become personally identified, and indeed, to reputation itself. Aging is often difficult, but it becomes even more challenging when we insist on hanging onto the world as we experienced it in our prime, when we keep grieving over the loss of the body and abilities we once had, or when we rage against our diminishing place in the world. Paradoxically, by hanging onto these disappearing things, we grow increasingly ridiculous, embittered, and toxic; resulting in even greater loss to our life and our relationships.*

Joy and influence lie in the opposite direction—in letting go of seasons that have ended, of people we cannot please, and of dreams that drive us to ignore life, friends, and God.

32

WHAT MATTERS MOST TO ME

(For my Children, Grandchildren, and Great Grandchildren)

Life is short, much shorter than I ever imagined. It seems I'm way too young to be old. It was only yesterday I was growing up in Bismarck, having fun with my friends in the neighborhood. I only thought about what was directly in front of me and didn't give much thought to take a long look at my world and the world around me. But now I've gained some perspective from James 4:14.

Yet you do not know what tomorrow will bring. What is your life? You are a mist that appears for a little time and then vanishes.

Here is what I've learned. If I seek after God with all of my heart, I will find him . . . and I did. If I honor God, He will honor me . . . and He did. God will give me the tools to accomplish what He has set out for me to do . . . and He did. I love what King Solomon said at the very end of Ecclesiastes: "Let us hear the conclusion of the whole matter: Fear God, and keep his commandments: for this is the whole duty of man."

I've had my share of difficulties in life, but God has delivered me from them all. He has been immeasurably gracious to me at every turn. Whether blindness or abuse, achievement or failure, joy or loss, cancer or vitality, family or friends, I have learned what I so often whisper to myself . . . God is near. Some may theorize about God's existence, but my faith is built on the undeniable consistency of His presence throughout my life. With that I cannot argue. I was created to be salt and light to everyone I meet or affect. To what measure is solely determined by the potency of my relationship with God.

We all take our own creative path, but it is God who promotes and brings the increase. That's important because it is here that we're defined. Not only by accomplishment, but also by how we respond to others in life. It is in our compassion, fairness, diligence, caring, kindness, gentleness, and peacemaking that we see who we are. My contentment is also born out of my authentic joy for the success of others.

My sole aim in life is to give my unequivocal excellence to the Creator of all things, in everything. For me, life is not about my significance, but solely for God's glory as He uses me for His purposes. This allows me to rest in His power and gives me great freedom

My friend, Bruce Koblish, once said, "Life has an energy and a mysticism of its own. God is the center of it." I like that word "mysticism." The word "mysticism" comes from the Greek *mystikos*, meaning "to conceal." God conceals stuff from us, so it's impossible to have answers to all of life's questions. The fact is; I really don't need resolution to most of my questions. I'll have plenty of answers . . . later. But for now, I'll keep looking to make a lasting difference in people's lives as I'm finishing the ride on this runaway horse.

There are far, far better things ahead than any we leave behind.

C.S. Lewis

REMEMBERING BISMARCK

- Baby Buffalo sundaes at Finney Drug
- Skiing at Twilight Hills
- Jerry's Supper Club
- The Hut
- The Seven Seas
- The Coffee Cup Café (Lydia Finlayson)
- Jack Lyon's hamburgers
- The smell of popcorn wafting from the concession stand at the basketball games in the World War Memorial building
- Football games at Hughes Junior High and St. Mary's Homecoming floats and bonfires
- Rodding Main Street
- Sgt. Mac Thompson
- Carmel rolls from A&B Pizza.
- Pizza burgers flying style, Hot n' Tots, Purple Cows, and Calypsos, from the Big Boy, Tartar burgers from Scotty's
- Listening to rock n roll from KOMA (50,000 watt station out of Oklahoma City)
- KFYR and KXMB television, KFYR and KBOM radio stations
- Cheeseburger platters, strawberry shortcake, and cheese frenchees at King's Food Hosts
- The presentation of "Messiah" at Trinity Lutheran during the Christmas season
- Ice skating rinks and warming houses
- The Capitol building lit up at Christmas

- Bismarck and St. Alexis hospitals
- The Provident building weather beacon
- Annual choir, band, and orchestra concerts in the winter and spring
- The presentation of "Gloria" at Bismarck High School
- The St. Mary's Carnival
- Mandan Rodeo
- Trail rides and hayrides
- Various church pancake dinners
- The aroma of Dakota Maid and Bismarck Bakery.
- Candy from Bashara's, Saba's and the OK Confectionary
- Fishing along the Missouri river
- Swimming at Elks Pool and going for a Dairy Queen or Lik-M-Aid from Sundahl's Jack and Jill grocery
- The B&R grocery
- Conrad Publishing (The Shopper)
- The Bismarck Tribune
- The Teen Club
- Eating at the Patterson Hotel
- Teen Canteen at Hillside Pool
- Parades down 4rth Street with the Bismarck and St. Mary's Bands marching
- The soda counter at Arrowhead Plaza Drug Store.
- Late nights at the Drumstick.
- Knoephle ("nefla") soup at Kroll's Kitchen.
- Onion rings and the garlic toast at The Gourmet House. Eating hamburgers and fries and watching The Fabulous Flippers and The Tradewind's 5 at the GP Hall of four Seasons
- The Dimensions
- Davey Bee and the Sonics
- Esky The Weather Wizard
- Dilly Bars
- The Elks Club and The Elks Club Band

- The El Zagel Plainsmen
- Sadie Hawkins Dances
- Junior Senior Prom
- School dances
- Sons of Norway lutefisk dinners
- DeMolay and Rainbow Girls
- Luther League and youth groups
- The Red Owl and National Tea
- City, college and high school theatrical and musical productions
- Civic Music and Thursday Music Club
- Pioneer Park parties
- The Sandbar
- Dakota Zoo
- The World War Memorial Bridge
- Firecracker stands between Bismarck and Mandan (The Strip)
- The "Pen" (penitentiary)
- Watching the beautiful costumes and ceremonial dances of various Native American groups
- The theater presentation of Custer and his soldiers at Fort Lincoln
- Saturday Circus
- Local television shows and the sign off patterns at night
- Double ditch

ACKNOWLEDGMENTS

When you publish a book or a recording, you are acutely aware that it is not accomplished by one person. I would like to thank my longtime friend and fellow creative, Beverly Mansfield, for her wise direction as she alleviated much of my trepidation throughout the process. I am grateful for having two brilliant editors in Darcie Clemens and Gwen Ellis. I am so thankful to Joel Porter for creating the book cover and to Mark Weising for his interior book design.

Book Supervision:
Beverly Mansfield (Owner) Chartwell Literary Group

Editors:
Darcie Clemens
Gwen Ellis (Seaside Creative Services)

Interior Book Design:
Mark Weising

Cover Design:
Joel Porter

@POPPIE'S HALLEL PUBLISHING

ABOUT THE AUTHOR

Greg Nelson is a Contemporary Christian producer, songwriter and orchestrator. He has produced recordings for Sandi Patty, Evie, Steve Green, Larnelle Harris, Wayne Watson, Twila Paris, Michael Crawford, and Richard Smallwood, including multiple artist recordings with Amy Grant, Michael W. Smith, Steven Curtis Chapman, Bebe and Cece Winans, Graham Kendrick, Jennifer Holiday, Kathie Lee Gifford, and the American Boychoir among others.

He has produced multiple gold and platinum recordings along with 20 Dove Awards and over 30 nominations. He has produced seven Grammy Award winning recordings with 13 nominations. He has received song, songwriter, and publisher awards from Broadcast Music Incorporated (BMI), the Nashville Songwriter's Association, and the Gospel Music Association. He received the BMI "Special Contribution Award" for his many outstanding efforts in the world of Christian music.

He was the third recipient of Gospel Music Association's "Impact Award" for his outstanding work and influence in the Contemporary Christian Music industry. His productions of The New Young Messiah, Emmanuel, and Hymns and Voices have been successful Christmas tours featuring many high profile artists.

In retirement, Greg is continues to write music, and has completed a suite for tenor soloist, treble voices, organ and strings entitled "The Hallel." He was commissioned to compose the music for a Christmas poem setting by David Bengtson for the Manitou singers at St. Olaf College. In addition he is completing a choral work centered around Holy Week called "The Passion." He has penned songs for a number of Christian artists as well as composing several hymns. His modern oratorio, Saviour, co-written with Bob Farrell, continues to be performed in the United States, Europe, and Russia.

Nelson speaks on subjects of songwriting, production and artistry at colleges and universities, mentoring young "creatives" in the U.S., Russia, India and Taiwan. He often travels to Russia to teach at the largest Christian music conference in Russia held in Moscow. Pam and Greg's most important work in these days is nurturing and being counsel to their children and grandchildren.

CPSIA information can be obtained
at www.ICGtesting.com
Printed in the USA
LVOW10s0808110717

540961LV00018B/678/P